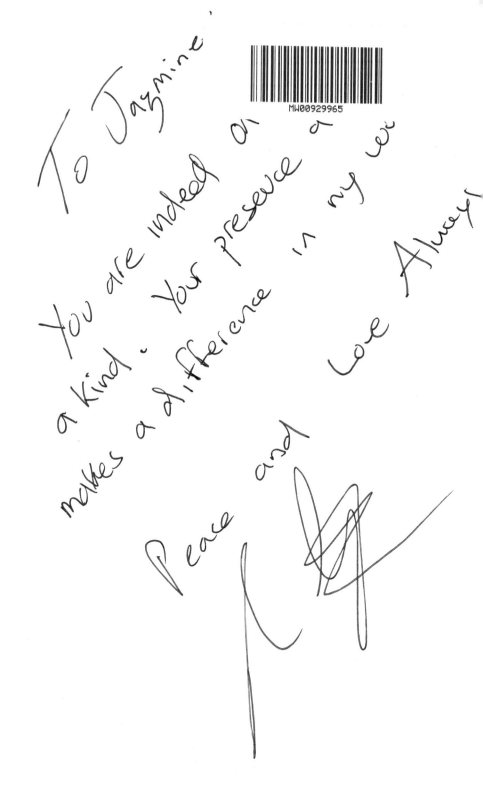

To Jazmine'

You are indeed on
a kind. Your presence
makes a difference in my life

Peace and

Love Always

THE
GREATER YOU
THE JOURNEY OF AWAKENING

DR. RUSSELL CLAYTON

BALBOA.
PRESS
A DIVISION OF HAY HOUSE

Balboa Press books may be ordered through booksellers or by contacting:

Balboa Press
A Division of Hay House
1663 Liberty Drive
Bloomington, IN 47403
www.balboapress.com
1 (877) 407-4847

Because of the dynamic nature of the Internet, any web addresses or links contained in this book may have changed since publication and may no longer be valid. The views expressed in this work are solely those of the author and do not necessarily reflect the views of the publisher, and the publisher hereby disclaims any responsibility for them.

The author of this book does not dispense medical advice or prescribe the use of any technique as a form of treatment for physical, emotional, or medical problems without the advice of a physician, either directly or indirectly. The intent of the author is only to offer information of a general nature to help you in your quest for emotional and spiritual well-being. In the event you use any of the information in this book for yourself, which is your constitutional right, the author and the publisher assume no responsibility for your actions.

Any people depicted in stock imagery provided by Thinkstock are models, and such images are being used for illustrative purposes only.
Certain stock imagery © Thinkstock.

Print information available on the last page.

ISBN: 978-1-5043-9225-9 (sc)
ISBN: 978-1-5043-9224-2 (hc)
ISBN: 978-1-5043-9226-6 (e)

Library of Congress Control Number: 2017918535

Balboa Press rev. date: 01/04/2018

CONTENTS

I dedicate this book, in loving memory, to my father, Russell Clayton Jones Sr., and my mother, Mamie Hozell Jones. They gave me life, and through this life, *The Greater You* was born.

I also dedicate this book to my children: Flynt, Quest, Nevaeh, and Kaya. My role as a father has awakened my own inner child. I thank each one of my children for being the amazing teachers that they are for me and for opening my heart to a love that I otherwise would never have known.

I also dedicate this book to all the children of the world. Our children are our future. May their hearts remain pure and their minds remain open to self-realization in their lifetime. To my loving wife, Olivia, who awakened the unconditional love in my being and without whom my journey of awakening would not have been possible.

MY INTENTION FOR
THE GREATER YOU

My intention for *The Greater You* is to create a ripple effect in the consciousness of all mankind. I desire to spark a global spiritual transformation that loving souls all around the world will feel. Let this moment be forever known as the birth of the greater you. A society rooted in love that honors every soul is the ideal universe of the future. May this tiny ripple continue to expand and spark a powerful shift in the frequency and evolution of greater human consciousness. My aim is that everyone who comes in contact with this book will experience an elevation in their consciousness, which will spark a shift in that person's identity from their ego mind to their heart. It is this inward movement that empowers the witness inside each of us. The discovery of your truth brings love, wisdom, understanding, joy, and purpose to all courageous enough to accept this journey.

PREFACE

The Greater You is a deep dive into the journey of awakening, which sheds light on the greatest questions of life. Who am I? What is my greater purpose? Where am I going? Why am I here? The answers to each of these questions lie dormant inside you. An awakened being discovers that love is the answer to all dilemmas of mankind. *The Greater You* is your companion guide intended to accompany you and your loved ones on the sacred journey of self-discovery. Use this resource over and over again. Embedded in each page are truths, insights, affirmations, prayers, and keys to support your awakening.

The Greater You is also a book that should be shared with your family, friends, partner, and children. The insights at the end of each chapter are meant to reinforce the most important principles discussed in each chapter. These poetic insights are intended to further elevate your mind and open your heart. The last insight in most chapters is an affirmation that is intended to be read aloud. Affirmations are powerful "I Am" statements that inject love, power, and purpose into your daily consciousness. When spoken, these affirmations come alive with the very vibration they were written from. Words can be impactful, but truth reverberates in your heart whenever you hear it.

I recommend reading the book in chapter order, but you may also make up your own order. If you are reading a particular chapter and find your mind drifting, try shifting ahead to another chapter that is more in tune with your vibration. For instance, if you are reading the chapter about crisis, but aren't connecting with it at the time, move on to another chapter. Perhaps you will resonate more with the love chapter. Find an association with the spiritual truths that resonate within you.

Be sure to note that the chapters you initially avoid are likely to contain the information you are resisting the most and therefore contain the insights that you need the most. Everyone has a soul, but there is only one spirit, the spirit of God, which speaks to us all. Spirituality is the universal language we all understand as the truth. Finding resonance within these passages is equivalent to finding the truth inside you. Please enjoy the book; it is meant to touch your mind, heart, and soul. *The Greater You* is meant to be read; but, more importantly, it is intended to be felt.

My inspiration for writing *The Greater You* came from my parents, Russell Clayton Jones Sr. and Mamie Hozell Jones. When I was growing up in Chicago, my mother was a kindergarten teacher. She taught me my core values, kindness, and the meaning of love. My father was a printer and a landlord. He was a quiet man of few words, but one whose strength and dedication was undeniable. He taught me the value of hard work and the importance of family. He had the dream to provide a private-school education for all three of his children, and he did. My sister Sylvia became a lawyer; my sister Cheri became a family therapist; and I became a physician. The practice of medicine taught me compassion and insight, and it bestowed on me the gift of healing. Little did I know that becoming a physician was only the beginning of my journey.

When my father transitioned in the year 1999, I was left feeling empty, and I longed for him. I searched for any writings from him or tape recordings of his voice, but all that remained were my memories of him. My love for writing and poetry slowly filled the void his loss had created. Writing became my passion. I was determined not to let history repeat itself, so I began to create a book of life for my four children to live by; *The Greater You* is that book.

To my surprise, what started out as a book intended only for my children turned into a manuscript on personal transformation for the whole world to enjoy. In hindsight, I can see that writing has been a catalyst for my own spiritual development. When I began to share my insights with others, I learned I wasn't alone in my journey. Clearly, my path was also the journey of many others. I theorized that if life was a process, then it could also be dissected, learned, and taught.

There are no coincidences; this book came to your attention for a reason. The connection between you and me has a greater purpose that will eventually unfold. We are all here on earth to evolve and connect with one another. My intention for *The Greater You* is that on any given day, you can open the book to any page and be inspired to live a more loving, abundant, and meaningful life. Thank you for the opportunity to connect with you. I love you all.

INTRODUCTION

There are two paths in life: an external path and a far-less-traveled internal path. Most of us pursue the external path because that is the way our parents showed us. The internal path is the journey of self-realization, the path to our truth. Much of our lives are filled with experiences that primarily serve to grow our ego-identity. We see ourselves through our accomplishments, travels, jobs, titles, and relationships. Furthermore, we see ourselves as separate from others, including our family, friends, and associates. We define ourselves based on our race, religion, gender, and social class. Most people see themselves as more valuable than their fellow man. Our elders teach us this way of separation, further distancing us from finding out who we really are.

The truth is that who we are is none of this. This identity crisis is the reason there are so many unhappy and unfulfilled people. For most of us, the path is that we are born, go to school, get a job, get married, have children, get old, and then die. Furthermore, if we are fortunate enough to have children, we send them on the same life trajectory as ours because that is the only path we have ever known. We are so busy living in personhood that we rarely identify with our larger nonphysical self. In reality, when we are caught up in ego, there is nothing but tragedy ahead. Anxiety, fear, and division are waiting for us there.

Personhood is the state of being where the consciousness gets stuck. This is where most people stay, and, eventually, where they die. The inner path is the journey of awakening, the relationship with your heart. Finding higher consciousness allows us to be joyful, liberated, and fully alive. Self-realization is the authentic search for one's truth. The truth is that you are a divine soul made from pure love—real love—not the love that goes looking for love. "A person is only a garment that consciousness wears for a while," Mooji once said. To know yourself as consciousness instead of as a person requires spiritual transformation. A shift of consciousness of epic proportions is required. This shift I am speaking of is from an ego mind-based identity to a soul-based identity. Our deeper nature is awareness itself; this is the dimension of the greater you.

Because you are reading these words right now, you sense there is something else beyond what you already know about this life. Soon you will need to make a choice for yourself to expand your mind to include the possibility of an awakening in you. Your transformation will bring about many life changes.

Remember that it will be easier to make changes in your belief system if your mental outlook is open, liquid, and soft. In contrast, when your mind hardens like cement, it becomes very difficult to change. I encourage you to remain open to the ideas, insights, and concepts in this book. While you may not agree with everything I present, stay open to all possibilities. Think of your life as a lump of clay. It's easier to shape the clay when it's soft and moldable. Likewise, with an open mind, spiritual transformation is possible for you in this lifetime.

In this era, there is a critical shift occurring where many souls are being called to evolve into light. Light is that part of your soul that is derived from Source. From this position, we will find joy, peace, and our higher purpose. We are all in the state of remembering. You are merely recalling what you have always known. Remembering is part of the process of self-discovery and the awakening to your true nature. Buddha said that "you are already the Buddha, already fully enlightened, you're merely just thinking that you are not." The Divine is already present; the Divine is within. This higher vibration is available to you right now. Your infinite soul is only one conscious breath away. Many people still feel they have to journey to faraway places, such as Tibet or India, to find consciousness. The truth is that you don't need to travel anywhere; consciousness already exists in you. The now is the main portal to higher consciousness available to you at this present moment.

Inside this book are nineteen chapters intended to spark and ignite your soul. Elevating your collective consciousness is critically necessary to make the journey inward. Transformation is the shift required to view yourself as the witness of your thoughts. As the witness, you'll begin to remember who you really are. The remaining journey you need to take will then become self-evident.

The first two chapters of *The Greater You* are about thought and emotion. These chapters serve to illuminate the power of your thoughts and make the connection to the emotions you feel. Your thoughts rule you. Positive thoughts lead to happy emotions. Fear and doubt are lower vibrational states that equate to resistance and lead to fear, anxiety, and depression. Your vibrational energy matters. Your thoughts determine your emotions, which subsequently determine your vibration and its matching energy field.

The chapter on energy provides reflections to raise your frequency and your state of being. The body-mind dynamic depends on your energy level. On the molecular level, movement, electricity, frequency, vibration, and flow states govern you. The awareness of seeing yourself in this way is beneficial to the process of your ultimate transition into light.

Scientists have determined that all living matter in the universe has a vibration. There is an inner energy field in the body consistent with your presence. Your inner and outer energy fields are different when you happily sense harmony. In this higher state, energy flows through you effortlessly and with little resistance. Everything that exists in the world, whether in solid or thought form, is energy. You are always vibrating in energy. Most people don't understand that everything is about vibration. The reason most of us don't understand vibration is that we have come to rely on the five physical senses of the body.

In this book, you will be called on to use your sixth sense: the power of intuition. Intuition is the language of your soul. The power of your inner being vibrates at a high and pure frequency. This force is otherwise known as Source. When I refer to Source or the Creator in this text, you can replace it with God, Buddha, Allah, Jehovah, the Supreme, Elohim, or Jah, depending on your personal beliefs. Source energy is both physical and nonphysical. "Source energy is the conscious energy that creates what we want in the nonphysical and we allow that into the physical, through our alignment with Source," Abraham Hicks wrote. When you are in vibrational alignment with Source, your energy is maximized. When you are in this universal alignment with your soul, you can effortlessly experience the high vibrational energy states of joy, love, and peace.

The chapters on intention and manifestation call on you to direct your life instead of being on the receiving end. By setting daily intentions, you purposefully create your reality each day. To be great at anything, you must put forth consistent effort and work. Grit is a key component of success. The more you practice setting daily intentions, the better you become at deliberate manifestation. Practice makes perfect. As you set your intentions, think of the process as adding purpose to your daily life. When you act purposefully, momentum is added to your flow, and your visions will begin to rapidly manifest.

Intentions are the spark needed to ignite the fire of all desires. Your future is unscripted; you are writing it in every single moment. Each choice you make influences the next moment, which in turn pushes your very evolution. You have the power to change the trajectory of your life, and you can go as high as your imagination will carry you. Visualize your desired future often, and focus your attention on what you intend to manifest. What you give your intention to grows. Don't worry about how or when it will happen; focus on your strongest desires, and your path will appear at your feet. Manifestation requires an intention, a vision, and your keen focus to come about. What you believe is what you receive.

The chapters on resistance and crisis aim to assist you in analyzing why you may not be getting what you want out of life. See your higher consciousness as a divine river within you. The river knows where it is going because it is the current of your soul. Your soul is the aspect of the Divine in you. Resistance to your inner flow is usually a thought process or behavior you're adding. In other words, you must become more aware of your destructive side, which dampens your flow and slows your progression.

Fear and self-doubt have cost many souls their dreams. The soul cannot experience fear. By remaining the witness of our experience in universal alignment, there is less resistance. When we learn to exchange our fear for faith, our reality has no choice but to serve us. Decreasing our resistance amounts to letting go and following the way of the soul. Your inner being uses intuition to speak to you and uses love to guide you. When you get out of your own way, the greater you can emerge.

Despite all our wishes to avoid the storms in our lives, they are unavoidable. Storms will come; that is the nature of life. But how we react to these storms is our choice. Everything in life happens for a reason or a season. If we reside in our center, we can see the storms of life as an opportunity to pivot and grow. Think of a pebble in a river. The torrential current shapes the pebble until it can find its proper place in the riverbed, thus delivering its higher purpose.

There is tremendous power in knowing that all storms will pass and that the sun will rise the following day. Life doesn't have to be a struggle. A crisis is more tolerable when you remain cool, calm, and collected. Peace and serenity bring acceptance and grace. Many times, your crisis is the very event in your life that transforms you into a more durable self. Following the path of least resistance allows one to navigate downstream in the river of consciousness. Your internal flow is increased the most by removing the resistance you are currently adding to your experience.

Your inner being is here to make a significant contribution to the world. You matter. Be fearless because you cannot drown. Your soul is both buoyant and storm resistant. *The Greater You* is a calling for your inner greatness to emerge. There is no situation you cannot survive; it is by the power of faith that all things are possible. Faith is the engine of your spiritual transformation.

The chapter on inspiration is a reminder of how powerful you are. Don't believe that part of you that says you aren't enough. Lack is a mind poison that distorts your perception of the truth. Be unstoppable. Be courageous, and reach deep inside your center where your power is unlimited. You are divine love itself, and you are indeed enough.

We maximize our power by maintaining our presence in the now. When you reside in the present moment, you can be joyful and free from the distraction of your thoughts. When the mind is quiet and the body is still, the portal of the now appears. You don't have to travel to find it; it is always right where you reside. Many people find it difficult to stay in the moment because the events of their past distract them and because they are anxious about the future. All fear, anxiety, and pain are dissolved in the now because it is a timeless dimension. Stay connected to this spiritual place, and you will discover the beautiful world of expansion. When you reside in the now, you have access to your power of creativity. All great ideas and things were created in the present moment.

The now is the portal to your soul, where you can find the realms of love, intuition, and inner vision. Your soul is always calling out to you. Your soul is that part of you that is timeless, limitless, and everlasting. The territory of the soul is pure awareness and serves as your inner identity. Qualities of your inner being are awareness, love, compassion, peace, and wisdom. When love and awareness come together, the door to the heart is opened.

The role of the witness is also a tool of your soul. "From the soul's vantage point you are coming home. From the ego's vantage point you are surrendering to love," Ram Dass wrote. In the chapter about the soul, there is further discussion on detaching from the ego mind and forming a greater identity with your nonphysical self. As you become more heart centered in your life and live from the elevation of your soul, you will attract the attention of others. They may not know why your energy is attracting them, but usually it's the brightness of the aura that surrounds you.

In the love chapter, you will be called on to embrace the unconditional love that resides in your heart. Love is the most powerful force in the universe, and its presence is a calling to come alive. Love is the state of being we all desire to return to. In the beginning, you were born as pure loving awareness. As a result of painful life experiences, we tend to forget who we truly are. Although the mind sometimes forgets, our hearts remain true. The journey of the heart requires you to give up old thought patterns that have held you back for so long. In spiritual transformation, your identity shifts away from ego identification to a heart-based consciousness. When you surrender to love, you will begin to experience a deeper love for your fellow man and see love in more of your experiences.

In my personal journey, the opening of my heart attracted the love of my beautiful wife, Olivia, into my life. Meeting my true love changed the trajectory of my journey. When you vibrate at the frequency of love, there is a healing that takes place in your life. Old wounds to your broken heart are healed, and you become a stronger and more durable being. Once the light of love illuminates it, your heart opens wider to those who are suffering. There is a sense of oneness that can be attributed only to the presence of love. Your loving awareness is a gift to share with those who are struggling to find their place in the world. True love radiates from your heart, and people around you cannot help but notice and be affected by it. There is no scenario that is resistant to the power of love.

To have a truly great journey, one must also serve others. Your life is a gift from heaven above. You are a light in the world, has and you have the innate ability to brighten the worlds of those around you. Your higher calling involves sharing your gifts in the service of all humanity. When compassion comes calling, answer the phone. Whenever you give unselfishly to others, you create a greater space for your own spiritual expansion. When you encounter a wounded soul, treat them with love and compassion. Your attention may be the very medicine that heals that soul and makes them feel whole again.

The chapters on gratitude and compassion stress the importance of being thankful for your very existence. When my job as a surgeon becomes overwhelming, I bring my focus inward toward gratitude. There is a tremendous amount of pain and suffering in the world, and the line that separates you from the other side is extremely thin. Your life can change in an instant. I'm sure you can think of a friend or acquaintance who has suffered a tremendous tragedy in one swift moment. You are here by the grace of God. As you take your next breath, fill your lungs with gratitude because somewhere on this planet, someone is drawing their last breath. Take the time to contemplate how fortunate you are for your very existence. You exist because you are blessed.

The chapter on well-being focuses on inviting an overall sense of wellness into your life. It is helpful to visualize yourself surrounded by an invisible giant umbrella of wellness. Believe all is well around you. You are right where you are supposed to be, and your path is always at your feet. Sometimes we take our gifts for granted and take on bad habits, such as overeating, smoking, abusing alcohol, being violent, or taking drugs. In our unconsciousness, we are unaware of the toxicity we take on because of our negative thinking or unconscious behavior. The body is the temple of the soul, and everyone gets only one body per lifetime.

Once you determine the journey of awakening is for you, you must take steps to eliminate unconscious thoughts, habits, and behaviors that have a negative impact on your life. This is a form of self-love. Part of the mastery of life has to do with the tailoring of your actions down to only those that actually serve you. Hold space for the concept of wellness in your life; you have nothing to lose and so much to gain.

The vital force in all living things is the thread that connects us all. This ever-changing universal field is as big as your imagination and is constantly expanding. This divine vibrational field serves as the stage of development and the maturation of your soul. The intelligence of the universe is the genesis of our creative ideas and the cradle of our dreams. You and the universe are one. The great beyond that physically surrounds you is also part of you. The seasonal patterns observed in nature stir comparisons with the spiritual transformation happening inside us as human beings.

The energy in nature is the same energy that flows through our bodies. That is why when we are in a forest or near the ocean, there is a calm to our presence. My favorite place to relax is the beach. It is the place where the roar of crashing waves drowns out my thoughts. If you are suffering, try taking a walk on a beach. When you look out toward the horizon, the waves of the ocean are too numerous to count. The grains of the sand on the beach are also incalculable. Therefore, the mind has no choice but to surrender to the state of silence, beauty, and pure presence. The energy of your natural surroundings invites stillness and peace in your very being. Nature is where you can forget about your problems and feel the loving embrace of all the splendor God has created. In nature, the seasonal changes of plants and wildlife are openly apparent. The moon transitions daily in its monthly cycle. The sun rises each morning, providing the light our eyes use to see.

Both man and the universe are alive with the vibrant presence of Source, but they are both susceptible to the effects of time; only the soul is ageless. The process of aging is a reflection of time. Over the years, many people suffer damaging effects from crisis after crisis in their lives. Some people show their age more than others. It is common for people to compliment each other by commenting on physical appearance in this regard. "Oh, she looks so good for her age." Still others appear weathered and beaten down by their tragic lives. In the body, the aging process spares no one, but those who maintain a childlike spirit and loving smile experience less damage from the effects of time.

The chapter about transformation discusses the internal shifts that happen in our lives to change our outlook and shift our frequency. Life is here to be experienced, and some experiences are bound to leave you shaken and disturbed. Many people never recover from a major crisis in their lives. Illnesses like cancer can cripple some people. For others, the crisis may be the loss of a parent or child. Regardless of the crisis, our challenge is to adjust our thinking and way of life in order to accept our circumstances—whatever they may be.

From the altitude of the greater you, you have the option of seeing yourself not as a body but as an infinite and everlasting soul. You may lose your memory one day, or perhaps you may lose a leg in an accident, but the real you is still there. The real you is the witness of your thoughts, emotions, and actions. The real you is the greater you, timeless and infinite. It is that part of you that lives beyond space and time. All that is born will one day die, but what is unborn cannot die.

Your soul was never born but gifted to you by the Creator. No part of the real you ever experiences death; your body merely transitions into spirit consciousness. Many philosophers theorize that all fear in mankind is based on the fear of dying. Truthfully, there is nothing to fear when the fate of each life is the transformation into pure love and light beyond the stratosphere, into another time and dimension. There is no such thing as death; you are merely returning home. The real you is the light of your very soul.

The chapter on the true self works to illuminate the characteristics of your divine nature. Beyond your reflection and your ego-identity lies your infinite self. Beyond words, lies, and deeds is your truth. As you peel away layer upon layer of misinformation and false beliefs, you get closer to your true identity: the self. Dr. Carol McLaughlin wrote, "Your story is not who you are. Your mind craves safety and security and it will create a story of who you are. But problems arise when you believe that you 'are' your story and that the story is true, complete and unchangeable." Our calling is to go beyond the identity linked to thought. A perfect Spirit, whose intelligence and power have no end, created you. The mind of God created you. The truth is that we are consciousness without the identity of the body mind.

The chapter on oneness is the journey that will carry you the full distance, beyond the parameters of time, to a state that is the embodiment of timelessness: a state known as oneness. You are a spark of the Divine amid activation. Oneness is the realization of the unity of all life, in which there is no separation from God. "You are not a drop in the ocean, you are the entire ocean in a drop," Rumi wrote. Separation is an illusion; everything is already one. The mind created separation under the direction of the ego. The ego is the main factor that tries to prevent you from achieving unification.

In discovering oneness, you will experience an identity shift from the ego to the level of the soul. Your five senses will be joined by an enhanced level of perception as your vibrational progression continues to accelerate. Unresolved emotional blockages and stagnant energies from your current and past lives will come to the surface, and you will be able to attain the clarity awakening offers. There is wisdom in clarity, and your vibration becomes that of calmness and serenity. There is peace in knowing who you really are. As your awareness continues to expand, you will become more sensitive to the worldwide human condition. As a more enlightened being, the door of compassion swings wide open.

You may find yourself quick to shed a tear at the site of suffering in your fellow man. Your soul deepens as the well of gratitude fills your daily life. As you spend more time awake in gratitude, you will spend less time asleep and in forgetfulness. At the level of society, there are forces present that try to separate mankind culturally into isolated pockets of humanity. The oneness in your heart and the expansion of your higher self will no longer tolerate the divisive forces of judgment, separation, and hatred. We are all interconnected, and the fate of one of us is tied to the fate of us all. When one soul rises, we all rise.

There is no set way by which beings come into awakening. For some, it is a gradual, slow burning off of the residue of the mind; for others, it is a metamorphosis that has been described as being on fire. Whatever way you may come into awakening, it cannot be given to you. *The Greater You* is a quest to become the best version of you that you can be. But, remember, you can't awaken simply by reading this book or any other book. Your journey is uniquely yours, and you must discover the hidden truth yourself.

This book contains nineteen chapters to ignite your soul, but you must go the rest of the way alone. You are the seeker of higher consciousness, and no two people's journeys are the same. Take comfort in knowing that the mere fact of your reading this type of book is proof that you are already on the journey to self-realization and the fulfillment of your highest potential. All the experiences that have happened to you in your present and past lives have led you to this point right now.

As we journey deeper into *The Greater You*, remember that the divine nature is inside every woman and man. If we label something as difficult to grasp or incomprehensible, then we will never grasp it. Open your mind to the idea of seeing the unseen and feeling what you have never felt before. Don't be discouraged if there is something you read that you don't understand. Even the greatest thinkers of all time have stood in awe of life itself. Be patient, and don't compare yourself to others and the pace they are traveling. You can go only at the rate you can go. I encourage you to go as far as you can, until you feel you are done.

Keep alive your focus and desire for awakening in this lifetime. When you experience periods of stagnation, don't be discouraged. Pauses are built-in periods for rest and reflection; you will soon be on your way again. All good things happen in time. The yearning for self-realization pulls a person into the journey of awakening.

Somewhere in our subconscious, there is a memory of something that comes from behind the veil. The call of the soul is a continuous whisper to awaken. Answering the call allows us to reach our full potential and uncover our higher purpose. In awakening, you are no longer dreaming, because you are no longer asleep. The journey of awakening is the discovery of your truth and your divine relationship with the Supreme.

As you begin to awaken, your psyche shifts with the realization that you are an infinite being. Your body deteriorates in accordance with time, but your soul is immortal and everlasting. Awakening is the spiritual evolution in which you remember that your life isn't separate from God. There is oneness in all beings because we are all from the same Source. There will be nothing to fear when you come into vibrational alignment with who you really are.

I request only one thing from you. Leave everything aside. Meet me with an open mind and no expectations or attachment to any of your prior beliefs. Meet me in the space of openness and vulnerability, where all possibilities arise, and let's see what happens there.

CHAPTER 1

Thought

The Power of Thought

The world has always put great emphasis on the power of thought. There have been many great thinkers in the history of the world; among them are Socrates, Plato, Einstein, Buddha, and Rumi. As children, we are taught to think harder and think for ourselves. However, while reading *The Greater You,* I would like you to entertain the concept of having no mind. Thought is the outcome of memory, and memory is the outcome of experience. Because your experience is always limited, so are your thoughts. To maintain a personal identity based on your thoughts is quite limiting. There is a space inside your being that is free of thought and infinitely more powerful than your mind. Your mind is quite busy offering constant thoughts, opinions, and judgments, which I call *mind noise.* The noise is never ending and offers little rest to your being. The practice of emptying your mind is beneficial. Practice emptying your mind of all thoughts of doubt, fear, and anxiety at least once a day. What you stand to gain is peace of mind. Emptying the mind is healing by nature; it refreshes the brain, raises energy levels, and stimulates brain neurons, which generate new, positive thoughts and in turn create positive events. This can be done by focusing solely on the breath. The only thing you must do in life is breathe. Breathe deeply, in silence, and feel the beat of your heart in your chest. Conscious breaths take you into the now and connect you with your inner being.

Meditation

Meditation is helpful in quieting your mind's noise interference. Meditation also puts you in a receptive mode that helps you become a better receiver of all that is good. In meditation, the mind is clear, relaxed, and inwardly focused. Meditation does not entail the suppression of your thoughts, but it does require that you notice them when they arise, and see them to be both coming and going. Try to remain as the observer of your thoughts, but do not attach your focus to any individual thought. Between every two individual thoughts that arise, there is an empty space. In this very space, we find the silence and the stillness necessary to experience the presence of our souls. The emptier our minds get, the more present we become. The benefits of meditation include: mindful breathing, less stress, profound relaxation, emotional stability, increased clarity, inner silence, higher consciousness, enhanced awareness and energy, and peace of mind.

The Vertical Dimension

The gap between two thoughts is where the vertical dimension lies. The vertical dimension is where the inner journey to the heart and soul can be found. This dimension of no thought remains undetectable until you turn your attention to it. When you focus your attention on this sacred space, the portal of the present moment opens and connects you to your inner power. The horizontal dimension is governed by time and space. This is where your thoughts predominate and where all questions and problems lie. To most people, this is their home. It is where they spend most of their lives and also where they die. Try this exercise to stretch your consciousness: Visualize the ripples on the surface of the ocean as the horizontal dimension. Now concentrate on becoming the wave itself; this brings your consciousness into the vertical dimension.

Personhood

In personhood, we experience thought as a way of standing apart among many others. Deep thinkers are often rewarded with important positions in corporations, leadership roles, enormous salaries, and great power. However, in the journey of self-realization, we must learn to silence the mind. Thinking our way into an enlightened state isn't possible; in fact, just the opposite is true. The more the mind generates thoughts, judgments, and solutions to validate its position, the farther away we move from alignment with our inner being.

People use words and thoughts to communicate their positions in reality as they see it. However, you aren't your story; you are an infinite spiritual being made in the mind of God. This identity confusion is responsible for virtually all anxiety, confusion, fear, and doubt. If you can shift your identity away from the ego mind to the consciousness, you can leave behind your lower mind and embrace your true nature. You are pure loving awareness, the unmanifested.

You Are Not Your Story

Although most people believe their stories are important, story is of little importance in this journey I am speaking about. One day in your future, everything you see before you will disappear, including your surroundings, body, and loved ones. Life in this earth reality is but a small speck of time on the calendar of forever. Contemplate the end of your life. What will your days be like when your story no longer has any value? You can't take your attachments with you into the afterlife. The most important relationship in existence is your relationship with your infinite self. This sacred relationship is beyond words, stories, space, and time. Why wait until your death to get to know your infinite soul when you can do so today? You have so much to gain and absolutely nothing to lose.

Your evolution of consciousness is about the journey from your mind to your higher self. Presence is the space where understanding, compassion, wisdom, and peace reside. You arrive at presence by practicing stillness, silence, and simply the joy of being. Words aren't necessary on this trip because your soul doesn't use the English language. Love is the language of the soul. If your purpose is to live a more meaningful life, then surely you have heard the call of your soul. Your soul is your glory, the part of you that is infinite and everlasting. Illusion happens whenever you hold the belief that your great journey is external and thus outside yourself. The truth is, your greatest journey is always inward.

The Power of Belief

We all have the inherent ability to cocreate our experience. This linear reality is largely based on our perception of ourselves. We become who we think we are. Our thoughts are tiny waves of energy, all carrying a certain vibration. When the mind meditates on a particular thought, that idea grows exponentially and morphs into a feeling or a belief. The stronger a certain belief is, the more likely it is to become a core belief. Our core beliefs shape and define our reality. The effect of each thought is determined by the intentions behind its sending force. The greater the power of belief behind your ideas, the more deeply they can penetrate the universe. This movement from a thought to its expression in physical reality is what I call "from the wave to the particle." Having a fundamental grasp on the idea that your thoughts create things is crucial to your understanding of the power of thought.

Humanity's first great discovery was recognizing that we could think. Our second great discovery was that something happens because of our thinking. It has been said that all of us are where we are because of what we're thinking. A single thought is capable of stopping an alcoholic from drinking, and you are one brilliant idea away from generating millions of dollars that could secure your financial future. Your thoughts contain energy, and they become stronger when the power of faith joins them.

Changing Your Mind-Set

What is inside you must come out. T. D. Jakes says, "You can't get greatness out of you if you are breathing in weakness." A multitude of positive thoughts are behind everything good in your life. The practice of positive thinking increases the yield of good outcomes. Your attitude is your mental approach to your life, toward yourself and others, and this creates your unique vibration. After all, your attitude determines your altitude in life. If your starting point is anxiety, confusion, or despair, you may want to change your mind-set. All confusion is rooted in the mind. Your mind-set is the set of beliefs you are currently operating from. It is useful to change your mind-set often; otherwise, you risk getting stuck in the land of old ideas and outdated beliefs that no longer serve you. Don't sail in the boat of your mind. You don't have to be the architect and designer of every aspect of your life; it is already unfolding exactly as it should.

The Importance of Thoughts

While you contemplate an existence beyond thought and words, it is still relevant to speak about the condition of your mind as it relates to daily life on earth. It is important to consider how you can use your mind more effectively to assist you in your spiritual development. We first learn the importance of our thoughts as children. Much of our childhoods are centered on using our minds to communicate our thoughts and needs. Effective communication helps us to function in our daily lives. Shortly after birth, we are blocked from remembering our true identities as infinite souls. Because of this forgetfulness, we seek shelter in building ego-identities that are both durable and resilient so that we can survive.

When I was a little boy growing up in Chicago's South Side, my jovial aunt Annie told me that her key to happiness was the practice of positive thinking. She often said, "Your thoughts rule you." I hold Aunt Annie in loving memory. Her loving words have echoed in my mind throughout my entire life and in many ways have led me to the insights revealed in this chapter. Thoughts are powerful bits of energy capable of attracting the right people, circumstances, and events that our consciousness desires.

While we are all faced with the challenge of silencing our thoughts, resting our minds is also necessary. A tired mind is prone to making unconscious choices. Getting the proper rest and nutrition is essential to recharging the brain, which then allows the mind and body to refresh themselves. Being fully present brings about greater clarity and insight. Because of your heightened level of awareness, you become a more effective translator of the language of your soul.

The mind is a bundle of thoughts.
The thoughts arise because there is the thinker.
The thinker is the ego.
The ego, if sought will automatically vanish.

—Ramana Maharshi

Despite our best efforts to stay in universal alignment, we sometimes fall into old patterns of resistance that hold us back. Ideas of limitation and self-doubt lower our vibrations. The way to get rid of limiting thought patterns is to use daily positive affirmations and prayers. Affirmations are not only for manifesting specific goals but also for encouraging a life filled with positivity and gratitude. If you are holding on to negative beliefs from your childhood, you may find it difficult to rewire your mind with positivity. Early childhood failures lead to trust issues in adulthood. Nevertheless, training your mind is necessary to achieve the visions of your higher self.

Prayer

Prayer is the privilege of dialogue with the Creator. We use prayer to clear our minds of negative thoughts. The purpose of prayer isn't to ask for things but to receive direction on how to reach our divine greatness. Prayer builds faith, increases power, and raises trust that everything will work out for the best. Some people today have given up hope in their lives, but I want to tell you that there is always room for prayer. God is always with you, and He is always listening. Miracles do exist, and our communication with God opens the door for miraculous healing to take place. Are you holding out for a miracle? Then claim it as if it is already done. When you ask for something to happen in your life, you open the possibility to receive it. Anything can be yours if you just believe.

Prayer also serves as an experience to bring people together in love, gratitude, compassion, and understanding for one another. Prayer is also an acknowledgment that there is a power greater than you, and it is a confirmation that you can use that power.

The Power of Thought

Every thought you consciously focus your attention on starts
to expand. Your mind processes each thought and produces a
chemical surge in your brain that generates an appropriate emotion
to match that thought. Thinking about someone or something not in
your physical presence is also capable of producing an emotion
that your body feels, as if that person or thing were actually there.
By this very light, we know that as we learn to master or minds, we can
deliberately choose our thoughts to bring about our desired emotions.

How Your Reality Is Constructed

Your reality is constructed of infinite, tiny manifestations of
your thoughts, desires, and fears. Your frequency is a
broadcast signal composed of the energy behind your thoughts.
Each of your conscious thoughts offers an oscillating vibration to
the universe. If you want to match someone's vibration, then you
must tune in to their individual frequency. The way you tune in to
someone's frequency is by listening to understand them, not to judge them.

What You Believe Is What You Receive

You always have a choice either to believe your thoughts or
to reject them. You are making these choices
each millisecond of every moment. What you believe is
what you receive. What you think, how you feel, and
how you live your life all reflect the way you are
shaping the divine light that flows through you.

All We Have Are Our Beliefs

All we have are our beliefs, but when we cling to certain beliefs that are untrue, they add resistance to our flow. To free ourselves, we must identify and let go of the thoughts holding us back. A breakthrough is when we exit a repetitive thought pattern based on old beliefs and come out on the opposite side, free of the thinking that put us there in the first place. If we don't awaken to the concept of letting go in this lifetime, we will die without ever knowing what we have missed. Spiritual growth leads to expansion of the soul. When we stay open to new schools of thought, we give birth to new worlds in our ever-expanding universe.

If You Believe in Infinite Possibilities

If you believe in infinite possibilities, commit to trying new things. New experiences expand our awareness and teach us the value of experiences over things. We can learn only from what we don't already know. When we travel outside our comfort zone, we learn how to adapt to our discomfort, which enhances our survival skills. Be spontaneous and joyful when possible. Joy is the emotion we feel when we are truly living in the moment. Live forward and don't look back. Don't let yesterday's news give you the blues. Your thoughts and experiences of today shape your circumstances and the world of tomorrow.

Believe It, and It Is Yours

Are you holding out for a miracle?
Then claim it as if it's already done. When you ask for something to happen in your life, you open the possibility to receive it. Anything can be yours if you just believe. A belief is the strongest form of thought. A belief is constructed by multiple threads of like-minded thoughts that, once bound together, become so powerful that they have the power to change your reality. Beliefs have the power to attract the right people and right circumstances into your life to bring forth your desired condition. Believe it, and it is yours.

Consciously Slow Down

When you rush into a burning building, you are going to get burned.
Consciously slow down your decision-making process to
absorb all the details of each situation you face. This step
allows you to absorb, analyze, and decide your fate one moment
at a time. Make sure you can always live with the consequences
of your decisions, because you can never run away from your past.

Fear Disrupts Your Vibration

Fear is an emotional reaction to the thoughts that
you are currently believing. Fear disrupts your vibrational
alignment, which hinders your joy and expansion. Fear is
false evidence appearing real. If you take the challenge to
always question the validity of your thoughts, then you can
eliminate many false notions you are holding on to.
Fear can exist only in the space we hold for it.

Exhale fear; inhale peace.

The World Is Not Against You

The world is not against you. The world you see
is your creation. This is your world. Your reality is
merely a response to what you are creating and what
you are currently believing. Discard disruptive thoughts
and allow them to dissipate away. Build on only the
thoughts that serve you. Have faith that your current
situation will work out in your favor. Failure isn't an
option, and God's divine grace is your inherent blessing.

CHAPTER 2

Emotion

Take Control of How You Feel

One of the greatest revelations of my spiritual journey was the realization that my thoughts determine how I feel. In addition, I discovered that by changing the focus of my thoughts, I could improve my attitude and frequency. As a teen, I attended the University of Chicago Laboratory School. I played on the basketball team and ran track. Back then, a game-winning shot or a victory on the track made me feel good. I believed that feeling good or bad was a direct result of my actions alone. Now I realize that the quality of my thoughts determines my happiness. Happiness is a vibration and depends on disposition, not a person's circumstances.

The law of attraction is always in effect. Choosing to focus on happy thoughts generates happy feelings, and choosing sad thoughts will bring on sadness. You also have the choice to remain neutral to the events that you witness; just decide how you would like to feel, and simply be that. Keeping a positive attitude is simple when you choose to focus on thoughts with a positive vibration.

Allow Your Emotions to Be a Guidance System

Allow your emotions to be a guidance system by which you control your energetic balance. Understanding that you can control your emotions is an important step in seeing yourself as a powerful cocreator of your experience. Your mood is always a measurement of the extent of your distance from alignment with Source energy.

You accomplish the first step of becoming the greater you by taking responsibility for how you feel. You are the master of your vibration. When you are sad, blaming others for your circumstances is extremely tempting. We often avoid facing ourselves. Take a look at your condition in the absence of the one who judges. Don't let your happiness be conditional on the behavior of others. No one can make you feel bad about yourself unless you give away your power.

Attachment

Many people strive to be rich in life and believe money and material things will bring them happiness, but exactly the opposite is true. Many wealthy people are quite miserable and have lost their smiles. Vast amounts of money frequently bring problems and struggles for power into people's lives. Meanwhile, some of the happiest people I have met in my life have been among the poorest. Along with money comes external power that is temporary and unstable. A fortunate person isn't the one who has the largest bank account but, rather, the one who is rich in love, wisdom, and understanding.

The road to happiness isn't the same as the road to riches. Attachment to material possessions builds a false sense of self-importance. You no longer need a partner, places, or possessions to make you happy when you are tapped into the stream of higher consciousness. True character is attained by building one's consciousness through hard work, practice, and faith. Selfishness consumes the vessel that contains it. When people are self-centered and cling to material things, they often become miserable and self-destructive. Conversely, when you are selfless and use your energy to assist others in need, thereby performing a service for humanity, you will enjoy a harvest of abundant joy and bliss.

Happiness Is a Mind-Set

Happiness is also a mind-set. You must choose happiness to experience it. To be truly happy, you must make peace with your past, anticipate the future with excitement, and, most importantly, stay in the now. The present moment is where joy is found. Practice getting into alignment with your mind, body, heart, and soul. Begin to sense and feel the power of oneness. In difficult times, stay in stillness for as long as possible. Initially, you may find it difficult to remain still because of your current unconscious state; however, in time, as you become more conscious, you will learn how to stay there with a keen focus. Be empty, silent, and still. In stillness lies the sacredness of your divine spirit. As soon as you align with the present moment, all resistance and struggle will dissolve. There is nothing wrong in the now; what is left behind is pure love and light.

During the course of our days, approximately half of our thoughts are negative, which leads to sadness. This illustrates the need to reduce the flow of our thoughts. Part of the practice of spirituality is silencing the mind. A helpful tool is to view your thoughts and emotions as clouds. They are continuously passing before you, and then they go beyond you. Try not to hang on to them; just let them come and go as they please. If you don't focus on a single thought or emotion, they will eventually pass by. The thoughts we choose to focus on expand. When a thought is joined by a belief, identity, or emotion, or when it is objectified, the thought is then strengthened and isn't easily discarded. Therefore, to raise our frequency, we must choose ideas and behaviors that bring the best out of us and that serve our needs and the needs of those around us.

Joy

Joy isn't an emotion; it is a state of being. Having an abundance of joy in your life is the result of detaching yourself from inward selfishness. The more you draw nearer to the eternal heart, the closer you are to awakening to the divine love within you. To reach and experience joy, you must work on removing your attachment to things that don't serve you. Awakening to joy in your heart is a gradual process of mastering the practice of love, kindness, gratitude, compassion, and surrender.

Decide How You Want to Feel

Fear, anxiety, and sadness come from the sense of being deprived of something you want and don't have. How you feel is the direct result of the thoughts you choose to focus on. You can deliberately change your emotional state by choosing to reside in present-moment awareness. Take a moment to celebrate the gift of your life. Gratitude arrives promptly when you are mindful of the miracle of your very breath. Your next breath isn't promised to you; many souls will take their last breath on earth in the next few seconds. You are indeed a miracle because you are alive and here.

In today's world, many people blame their boss or work environment for their unhappiness. Many workers fantasize about changing jobs and finding peace elsewhere. No matter how stressed out you are now, I want to tell you that peace is available to you right now. If you are struggling to achieve happiness at work, try changing how you do your job. *How* you do something is more important than *what* you are doing. You can be a more productive employee if you can just inject pride and a winning attitude into your work persona.

The Practice of Smiling

Keep a positive mind-set. Smile more often; smiling releases neurotransmitters, called *endorphins,* from the brain. These endorphins brighten your mood. The more we stimulate our brains to release these neurotransmitters, the more relaxed and happy we feel. According to *Parenting & Family,* a baby smiles four hundred times a day, while an adult smiles eight times a day. Stress is the number-one reason why we lose our natural state and smile less. The practice of smiling has been shown to reduce stress by lowering cortisol levels. Smiling also makes people look younger because it lifts the face, and several studies have shown that smiling faces are seen as more attractive. When you smile at people, 50 percent of them smile back; this fact proves that smiling is literally contagious. This spreads the health rewards of smiling to those around you, and these benefits will come back to you. A smile from someone is a gift from their soul. Whenever you flash your smile, trace it back to its source at the center of your being. What is truly transferable is your smile and your energy. Similar effects are noted with laughter.

Laughter

Laughter is contagious, and, like smiling, it sparks endorphin levels. In fact, many yoga studios now offer laugh yoga, in which participants enjoy laughter for twenty minutes in order to feel better and enjoy its health benefits. Laughter is a powerful antidote to stress, pain, and conflict. Nothing works faster or is more dependable in bringing your mind and body back into balance than a good laugh. The day-to-day stresses of our environments demand that we find tools and exercises to counterbalance negativity. Laughter is a strong equalizer in balancing our daily emotions.

Neurotransmitters

In today's world, there is a tremendous amount of scientific research focused on pleasure chemicals, known as *neurotransmitters* (NTs). These polypeptides relay messages in the brain from neuron to neuron. NTs are extremely important in brain function; without them you couldn't think or feel. Neurotransmitters are polypeptides that are very important in bringing forth your emotions. Psychiatric medications work by altering these same chemical compounds in your body mind. When a thought is activated in your brain, it is spontaneously attached to an emotion. The brain then colors your emotions with a feeling—unpleasant, pleasant, or indifferent. You tend to avoid what is unpleasant and seek to approach what is pleasant. To what you are neutral to, you are unmoved.

Types of Neurotransmitters

Dopamine: Involved in pleasure and sexual functioning. It is involved with motivation, mood, attention, and rewards.

Norepinephrine: Functions as an antidepressant, regulates sleep, and affects mood and digestion. Most antidepressants aim at increasing its effects.

Serotonin: Functions as an antidepressant and regulates sleep, mood, and digestion. Most antidepressants aim at increasing its effects.

Acetylcholine: Promotes wakefulness and learning, and it is responsible for sudden bursts of tears.

Gaba: Helps one achieve a great sleep. It has antianxiety and pain-relieving effects. It enhances calmness and is the benzodiazepine receptor for drugs like Valium.

Oxytocin: Associated with closeness and blissfulness. It is commonly referred to as the love and bliss hormone.

Chasing Bliss

Worldwide usage of mind-altering drugs like marijuana, magic mushrooms, LSD, ecstasy, and ayahuasca has remained popular as a result of people's fixation with chasing bliss. People are now capable of purchasing small doses of happiness in the form of a plant, pill, powder, or experience. Alternative music festivals, such as Burning Man and Coachella, are capable of delivering mind-blowing neurobiological and auditory experiences capable of equaling any psychedelic drug experience. In the end, we must be careful not to become addicted to happiness itself and treat it as if it were a drug. We must be careful not to seek chemical solutions to our spiritual problems. Don't chase excitement, it will only end in suffering. What goes up must eventually come down. Instead, follow your ever-flowing natural state of bliss, the essence of what you are. It is possible to live passionately without pleasure seeking behavior. The difference between passion and excitement is that excitement always ends, and passion can be sustained. Be filled with a passion for good, for love, and for life itself. Put an end to your chase for excitement and relax into the present moment which is always sufficient. Our problems are here for a reason. Our sadness isn't here just to be washed away by the rush of pleasure. We must face up to our sad feelings as well. We are multidimensional beings capable of experiencing sadness and happiness at the same time.

Sadness

We are programmed to seek happiness. We avoid unpleasant emotions and seek experiences that make us feel good. In general, the motto is: what makes me happy must be good for me, and what makes me sad I choose to avoid. The trouble with this approach is that sadness is the very emotion we use to measure our happiness against. In truth, we need both emotions. Happiness and sadness both have the power to accelerate our spiritual growth. Profound change always has a pivot point, and these two emotions certainly qualify as game changers.

Invite your sadness to sit with you, and be curious about why it has come to visit you. Sadness points out aspects of yourself most in need of your loving attention. Ask yourself why you're feeling the blues and then try to get at the root cause. When you begin to have the answers to these questions, you won't need to look far for happiness; it will have already spontaneously arrived. Positive vibrations are everywhere, even somewhere inside a dark moment. There is always a glimmer of hope, a seed of encouragement, and an opportunity in which love is allowed to arrive.

The Practice of Kindness

One of the most powerful cures for a dark mood is the practice of kindness. The next time you seek to elevate your mood, put a smile on your face and start saying "hello," "thank you," and "please" throughout your encounters. As you spread kindness to others, your disposition will begin to elevate to higher levels. Soon you won't be able to remember why you were so sad. The practice of kindness shifts moods, elevates energy, and attracts goodwill. Our world is truly in need of a global healing and could use a few more smiles and laughs to spread happiness and kindness to all of humanity. Be an ambassador of joy in the world. Share your light with those who need it the most.

Your Mood

Your mood doesn't have to match your circumstances.
The greatness of your inner power allows you to redirect
your emotions to those you prefer, despite the presence
of any adverse conditions. Stay confident when staring into
the eyes of adversity. Let your attitude always reflect your
positive light and loving spirit. Your circumstances are
sure to change, but your vibration is always your choice.

Take Charge of How You Feel

Take charge of how you feel.
Be honest with yourself about how you are feeling
at this very moment. Gauge your current emotions;
decide how you want to feel, and simply be that.
Don't let your happiness be conditional on the
behavior of others. Feeling good or bad is about
how you're relating to your higher self.

Happiness Is a Choice

Your emotions are the primary driving force behind all your
manifestations. What all human beings desire is happiness. It is our
pursuit of happiness that drives our experience. All of your feelings are
related to either the presence of, or absence of emotion.
Happiness isn't determined by what is happening around you;
it comes from what is happening inside you.
Happiness is a choice; if you are unhappy, then change your thoughts.
When you choose to think joyful thoughts, neurotransmitters are
instantly released from your brain and flood your bloodstream,
creating a feeling of euphoria. Choose happiness. Choose love.

Your Emotions Are a Guidance System

Based on the law of attraction, whatever vibration you hold is subsequently mirrored in your life. If you are happy, then happiness will follow you. If you are anxious, then anxiety will find you. Sadness will create more sad situations to feel sad about. Remember that your emotions are in fact a guidance system designed to guide you through life. Take note of your emotions throughout the day and remind yourself that you are not your circumstances. Surround yourself with people and environments that bring happiness to you. When you experience negative vibrations, redirect yourself. Keep your positive energy flowing. Tune in to your higher mind and trust that your higher self will make the correct conscious choices in your life.

Happiness Is an Inside Job

The sadness you feel inside is a measurement of the distance you occupy away from the greater you. When you feel sad, it is because you have strayed away from your inner being. Your divine soul is your glory; be still in it and reside there. The alignment of your mind and body with your loving soul opens inner pathways of joy, wisdom, and energy inside your heart. Happiness is an inside job.

It's Okay to Be Where You Are Right Now

It's okay to be where you are right now.
It's okay to be less than perfect.
It's okay to be scarred. Your scars are
the very wounds that create wisdom.
It's okay to cry tears; your tears contribute to the
emotional current that navigates your very soul.
It's okay to experience joy, because you are indeed worthy.
It's okay to dream, because your dreams of today create
your reality of tomorrow.

Your Soul Is Born from Source Energy

Your soul is born from pure Source energy,
and it contains the whole consciousness of the universe.
Within this construct, abundance is always available to you.
Shortage consciousness is an anomaly that man has created.
It is supported by the belief that there is a lack of abundance
surrounding you. When we free ourselves of a shortage of
consciousness, we allow the paths of love, energy, and creativity
to flourish. Open your heart and mind to reclaim your inherent
gifts, and welcome pure joy and happiness into your life.

The Great River Within

The path of least resistance is always calm and easy.
The land of joy and fulfillment is our destination. We
can find our inner flow in each and every moment by
following our bliss. Opposite emotions, such as heartache,
irritability, fear, and self-doubt, are measurements of the
resistance you are adding to your flow. Without what
you are adding to it, there is often little obstruction to the
current of your flow. The great river of consciousness
running inside you is where you will find the
greater you and the awesome power of your soul.

Open the Path That Self-Love Creates

Far too many times, we fall short of the expectations
we set for ourselves. We beat ourselves up over what we
haven't accomplished, instead of celebrating our wonderful
achievements. This attitude alters our mood set point and stifles
our growth. Choose today to celebrate your accomplishments
and open the pathway that self-love creates.

CHAPTER 3

Energy Fields and Vibrations

Particles and Wave Forms

Have you ever felt energy projecting outward from another person? Perhaps you did when you walked into a room or a party. A person's dark energy may cause you to cross to the other side of the street, as a negative example. A positive example would be when you have the urge to smile or say hello to a perfect stranger. Your perception of other beings' energy fields is happening with each encounter in your daily life.

When I first laid eyes on my wife, Olivia, her presence captivated me. As I saw her standing there, there seemed to be a glow around her physical form, a vibrant field of beauty, color, and grace. It was truly something to behold. Because of what I saw and felt, I approached her with a simple "hello." That single utterance of hello changed my entire life. We are here to connect with one another. Don't be afraid to initiate conversation or pleasantries with people when you feel a strong urge to engage with them. You never know what can happen when you take a chance in life.

Auras

The colorful and vibrant outer energy field of a human being is called an *aura*. The auric field is a set of energy bands that graduate in frequency and color as they move outward from the body. Auras can be seen emanating from people, places, or things. Scientists have discovered that the color bands of a human aura actually pulsate and change according to a person's emotional, mental, and physical states. The brightness of your personal aura is ever changing and reflects your inner light. You are energy personified, and your outer energy always reflects your inner energy field, which is also known as *chi*.

Chi

Chi is considered the source of all movement in the body and the universe. In its intelligent state, it actually links our bodies with our souls. As such, it is often connected and associated with our breath and is seen as a source of vitality. To East Indians, chi is known as *prana*. When you breathe, you take in *prana*, a yogic word that means "life force." You take in oxygen too, of course, but also an ultimate vibration that is essential to living. This vital force is the force of the universe. It is well known that breath is the fastest way to change your energy pattern. Conscious breathing centers you and brings you into the now. All of us have felt our chi before; we just didn't know what it was.

Chi travels through the body by two paths: friction and sensation. When you are scared, you sense goose bumps on your body, and the hairs on your arms and the back of your neck stand up. This is visual proof of your chi. The martial art tai chi harnesses the power of chi to produce powerful physical force to use in self-defense. More commonly, ordinary people have found incredible strength to do superhuman feats when faced with danger or survival. This is an example of the raw potential power of chi in the body.

Everything is energy; in fact, the entire universe is alive with cosmic energy. Chi is formless and limitless, and it's the universal life force that binds everything together, including our solar system and the universe. This divine energy runs through your body and in all things. The great energy that spins the earth on its axis and propels it to revolve around the sun is the same energy inside you. Even the smallest particle in your body, an atom, vibrates with a divine spark.

Cosmic Energy

Cosmic energy, the essence behind all creation, is constantly moving and expanding. As human beings, we absorb our energy from Source. The source of cosmic energy is the Creator of all there is, the power of God. When we embrace knowing that the same energy that created this majestic universe is also inside us, a great power arises. As humans, we access our greatest power from the realization that we are a spark of the Divine. Cosmic energy is also what governs your mind to think. Your thoughts are waves of energy that each carry a vibration. Your thoughts are intimately linked to your emotions, which also translate to vibrational energy. What you think and how you feel determines your vibration.

Frequency

Your personal vibration is called your *frequency*. High-frequency energy activates positive emotions, and low-frequency energy activates negative emotions. The energy you currently emit is your point of attraction. Regardless of the state of being you are in right now, the law of attraction will add divine momentum to it. Be joyful, and joy will follow you. Live and let live, love and be loved. Low frequencies cannot exist in a field of high-frequency energy and awareness. Since life is constantly changing, it is normal to shift back and forth many times a day. Remaining the witness of your experience allows you to see and feel the energy that is arising from you. Positive thoughts and emotions expand your energy field, while limiting thoughts and emotions constrict it. Real change and self-realization happen from increasing your awareness of what is happening inside you at all times.

Many people I talk to are trying to find ways to remain in their high-frequency state for longer periods of time. The key to shifting out of low-frequency states is to get out of your mind and shift into alignment with your soul. Centering yourself allows you achieves stability. You can always get into alignment by being mindful and connecting with your breathing. Mindfulness is paying attention to what is arising in you in the present moment without clinging to it. Conscious breaths usher us into alignment with the now, where it is possible to leave fear, anxiety, and depression behind. Low-energy states usually result from looking too far into the future or focusing on a memory from your painful past. The present moment is a timeless and spaceless dimension of infinite potential. To live in the moment is to be joyful and to be free.

Stay centered and present as long as possible, and when you notice yourself drifting out of alignment, simply draw your attention back into the present moment. Your attention to this moment is all that matters. The now is where you can always find an abundance of peace, happiness, and balance. Your positive vibrational alignment can be a challenge to maintain for long periods of time. When you are on the spiritual path, you have the innate ability to recharge your spirit. The practice of kindness and gratitude instantly recharges your energy levels and shifts you back into alignment. Rejoice in the gratitude of life; your very presence is a miracle indeed. Be grateful for your existence and live each day as if it's your last.

Protect Your Alignment

According to Wikipedia, the world population as of March 2017 is estimated at 7.49 billion. All human beings carry their own vibration with them wherever they go. Proximity to those operating at lower frequencies can negatively affect our vibrations. When it is your intuition to distance yourself from someone, follow your instincts and don't be afraid to protect your alignment by simply walking away; this is a form of self-preservation. Don't let sleeping souls hold you back from spreading your wings and rising from the ashes like a phoenix. Rise up to the land of tomorrow and into the newfound era of the greater you. There is nothing that can stop you from evolving into light, and there is no one who can prevent your heavenly transformation from happening here on earth.

Try to surround yourself with beings who carry a positive vibration. This is the true essence of compatibility. Practical wisdom suggests that you become an aspect of the company you keep. The best means to connect with someone is to listen to them without interruption. The way you tune in to someone's frequency is to listen to them from a place of compassion, understanding, and love. When the ego is listening, we are only gathering information. When love is listening, we connect heart-to-heart.

Some people will not accept you in your fully realized state. Not because they don't like you, but because they are not yet comfortable with being vulnerable themselves. Some people are just not ready to meet you on this level of intimacy, and they will be uncomfortable with your new vibration. As an awakened soul, you have the ability to respond to every person with a deep sense of empathy and presence. Awakened or not, all beings are to be respected and treated equally.

Karma

Part of your soul's energy is your karma. Karma is the balancing of energy to assist in healing the soul. In this profound way, we are held responsible for every thought, feeling, action, or intention in this life and in past incarnations. For every action, there is an equal and opposite reaction, a natural law of the universe. By this light, you receive from the world what you give to the world. Karma teaches us responsibility and nonjudgment. Since we cannot know what is being healed through each event and what karmic debts are coming to conclusion, we cannot judge the events we see.

Flow

When a soul is highly focused and performing a creative task, one enters what author Mihaly Csikszentmihali refers to as the "flow state." This high-energy altered state is optimal consciousness resulting in optimal performance. This phenomenon is commonly seen in music and athletics when a performer is in "the zone." While in the flow state, humans are capable of amazing feats. Best of all, it seems to happen easily and in harmony with the environment. People in the flow state describe it as being on automatic pilot. There is a sense of ecstasy for the performer, since this person is doing what they love to do. Flow is also accompanied by a sense of timelessness and great inner clarity. While these periods of being in flow are amazing, they don't usually last for long periods of time. Next-level high-functioning flow states can be learned and activated on demand to manifest our greatness and be used to deliver our higher purpose.

As a surgeon, I often find myself in the flow state while performing an operation. Many times, during difficult operations, I have experienced the passing of several hours in what felt like only a few minutes. There is a sense of serenity and calm that emanates from my perspective as the witness, and I am able to sustain it throughout certain entire procedures. Many times, when I complete a surgery, I feel an exhilaration that can only be described as a wave of pure bliss. No matter what your job is, I am sure you have bursts of peak performances. Be aware of the existence of the flow state in you. If you can connect these moments of excellence and bliss, you may be looking at your key to maintaining an optimal state of peace, abundance, and joy in your life.

Life is all about energy. What matters most is the frequency of your broadcast signal, the intention behind the vibration you are sending out into the world, and the depth of your inner knowing that love is the answer to all of life's most important questions. Now that you are aware of the cosmic energy surrounding you, you undoubtedly feel a force you have never experienced before. You are born anew. Welcome to the greater you. The world is awaiting your highest energetic contribution. In some way, directly or indirectly, each one of us is changing the world.

The Many Reflections of You

The many reflections of your personality display the many
dimensions of you. What others see in you is only a fraction of
your true power. You have the capacity to accomplish anything
you set your mind to. The only limitations you have are the
ones you are currently believing. When we allow self-doubt
to flourish, we fall victim to our greatest enemy: our minds.
What we believe is what we receive. With faith we pray,
in God we trust, and by the power of love, we move.

Your Aura Is an Energy Field

Like a shadow that changes its length throughout
the day, your aura is always changing its colors, form,
and dimensions. This beautiful photoelectric field of
vibrational energy is always around you. Healers can deliver
energy to this hollowed-out space, based on intention. Your aura
is your personal energy field, an individual electromagnetic
presence that emits bright photons of love and light,
your heart's expression of your very truth revealed.

Love Is the Center of Your Universe

Relax; you don't have to worry about anything.
Your soul is infinite and everlasting. You possess a
life force that creates worlds and lights up the human race.
Your inner power supply of pure Source energy cannot
ever be stolen or destroyed. Your body is made of
star stuff straight from heaven. Fusion is the process
that fuels the sun, and love is the center of your universe.

Good Karma

When you have received favor but along the way have
accomplished your success with a cold-blooded, empty heart,
karma will find you. It is impossible to escape your karma.
Our mission as human beings is measured by how deeply we love
and are loved. An open heart is a vessel that can be filled with
an infinite amount of love, but deeds done with an empty heart
are destined to come back to you and drain your heart and soul.
To serve karma, you must repay good karma to others.

Protect Your Alignment

Don't let the negative attitude of others throw you out
of your alignment. Their attitude belongs to them, not you.
You are merely a trigger for their own unresolved issues.
Don't react or respond negatively to them. Bless them
and stay in your positive alignment. Love and teach.
Bless and be blessed.

Becoming a More Powerful Spirit Is Easy

Becoming a more powerful spirit is easy.
First, set the intention to increase your inner power.
Then, visualize yourself as the powerful cocreator of your reality.
The process of visualization is the ultimate basis for transformation.
What you think, what you say, and what you do all carry vibration.
Speak from the love in your heart and the kindness of your soul.
Just by taking these measures, you have increased your
inner power and become a more powerful spirit.

Take Back Your Power

Blame is a game people play.
When you blame others for your situation, you give away
your power. It is disempowering to believe someone else
could have more control than you in the direction of your life.
The only way someone can take over your life is if you give your
power away. When we blame others for our circumstances, we are
unable to receive the gifts wrapped inside our problems. The truth
is that we all have an obligation to ensure the materialization of
our dreams; this is known as empowerment. Empowerment
entails accepting responsibility for your current situation.
Take back your power today. The only person who can
keep you away from your dreams is you.

An Open Heart Creates Positive Flow

The heart is the regulator of our energetic state.
Think about what it's like to feel love in your heart.
The feeling is exhilarating; no other feeling compares.
The heart is also the root of the soul. The heart controls
your energy flow by opening and closing like a valve.
An open heart creates positive flow and allows kinetic energy to
pass through you freely. A closed heart creates an obstruction
in your flow. When a blockage forms in your heart space,
negativity accumulates inside you, resulting in sadness, stress,
anxiety, and disease. The heart is the center of our being,
the location of endless love, and the home of the soul.

Love Heals

(Read aloud)
I am going to create an energy burst,
and aim it directly at my own heart.
Designed to repair and heal my broken heart,
may it transform my pain into love and turn
my fears into faith. We are all healers.
When we love ourselves enough, there is
no dream that is impossible to reach.
Love heals.

CHAPTER 4

Consciousness

The Spiritual Path

Throughout my teenage years, powerful thought leaders of the world who exhibited a higher consciousness fascinated me. I learned of the life of Jesus, who gave his life to spread the word of God. I loved the story of Buddha, who is said to have attained enlightenment at age thirty-five. I greatly admired Dr. Martin Luther King Jr., Mahatma Gandhi, Nelson Mandela, and the Dalai Lama. To me, as a black youth growing up in the South Side of Chicago in the 1960s, the possibility of enlightenment seemed unrealistic, unattainable, and virtually impossible. As an adult, I learned that the spiritual path requires faith, dedication, vulnerability, compassion, practice, and understanding. My practice included reading hundreds of books written about the spiritual path. The more I read, the more I learned—and the more tangible the dream of awakening became.

My early readings included *The Celestine Prophecy,* by James Redfield; *Flow,* by Mihaly Csikszentmihali; *Be Free Where You Are,* by Thich Nhat Hanh; and *The Power of Now,* by Eckhart Tolle. There are many ways for souls to reach higher consciousness. My reading exposed me to fully realized authors who had already discovered their own inner truth. Although it is not possible to awaken from knowledge alone, I gained greater confidence from seeing the success of others, which inspired me to continue my journey. From my research, I was able to visualize a blueprint of the journey of awakening. I became a seeker of enlightenment, and from that point on, my inner fire of transformation burned brighter each and every day.

Love Consciousness

Love is the most powerful force in the universe; it changes people and scenarios. In my personal journey, love changed my life's trajectory and welcomed clarity into the space where there once had been doubt. My eventual awakening was the end result of my surrender to love. As I surrendered my heart to Olivia, the love of my life, I traveled to the deeper realms of my soul. We pledged an undying love for one another, and once we were united in purpose, our love moved to a new depth every day. In surrender, one removes all obstacles, both imagined and real, and dives into the abyss of love itself. Love is a bottomless well of divine vibrations that infuses the heart and mind with kindness, gratitude, and purpose.

The Power of "I Am"

Spiritual consciousness is a deep awareness of God within you. God has deposited love at the center of you and every other being— that is spiritual law. High-level awareness of your loving soul is the awakening of deep consciousness. Life is spiritual—nothing more and nothing less. By the power of the Creator, your path is illuminated by His divine light. God realization within you is the culmination of the journey of awakening. You are a child of God, made from divine love, and you have been blessed with a loving soul filled with the gifts of creativity and observation. Try to observe your divine intelligence, which is not put together by your thoughts. When we say, "I am conscious," it means, "I am conscious of everything happening around me."

The phrase "I Am" is universally accepted to describe the name of God. It can best be understood by defining *I* and *Am* separately. *I* refers to God or consciousness itself. *Am* translates as "to be" or "to exist." Therefore, "I Am" simply means "I, the consciousness, exist." This is the divine nature we are all born into. Before your name or job title, you are the "I Am" presence, a divine emanation of God. Every time you say "I Am," you are announcing the presence of God within you. Be careful what you attach "I Am" to, because it has the power to limit you or to free you.

"I Am" is really just the purest form of *I*, the beingness, your existence itself. This is your natural state. Most people's version of *I* is a three-dimensional version of themselves, which is only a shallow version of who they are. The real you is the pure space that has no past or future. This pure space doesn't rely on thoughts, emotions, memories, or images—it just is. The godly principle of each sentient being has no name, gender, religion, or agenda but just an unassimilated presence. The greatest and ultimate realization in life occurs with the realization that "there is only God."

Everyone wants to talk about *I,* but the aspect of you that I am referring to is to is the key here. The real you is unchangeable. You have taken your beliefs and attached them to a physical identity, which is really just a story based on your conditioning; because this version leaves you with a feeling of worth, you believe your story. You have bought the notion that you are a body with a soul rather than an infinite being inside a body. The truth is that you are primarily the soul that survives the physical death of the body.

The Dimension of the Greater You

Matter is anything that has mass and takes up space. Matter is composed of molecules and atoms, which in turn are composed of protons, neutrons, and electrons. This energy field of subatomic particles in normal matter is so dense that it appears solid, but it is not. This seemingly solid state is an illusion. Even a rock or a tree is actually a moving stream of energy particles. In between each moving particle are empty spaces that, together, form the background of our existence. Similarly, the human body also contains a vast amount of empty space. There is a space inside every atom and in between every molecule of your body. A hydrogen atom is 99.9% empty space. Your dimension of inner space emits energy, and, much like the space in the universe, it is constantly moving and expanding. This space is your center, the source of your divine light. This dimension is beyond space and time, and is continuously growing and evolving beyond the speed of light. Consciousness travels inside each soul at the speed of love.

Your inner space is a time-free dimension where freedom, joy, and peace can be found. It is there for you right now. Jump into alignment with your soul. When you learn to silence your ego mind and become more comfortable in stillness, your soul awakens. In time, you will become more aware of this silent and powerful sense of presence. The thinker of your thoughts is the ego, and it is your challenge to remain the witness behind your thoughts. Feel the presence of your inner being, and you will discover the awesome dimension of the greater you. The action of inward observation activates your talents of understanding and insight. Understanding can only take place when the mind is quiet. In stillness you can observe your thinking and your reactions to what is happening for you. Sit quietly without any motive or intention, and don't use any effort to try to achieve anything.

As you become more accustomed to accessing the presence of your soul on a regular basis, you will begin to see yourself more as a nonphysical presence than a physical entity. More than ever before, you will find yourself around other like-minded people, and you will crave more interactions with wise and enlightened souls. With increasing frequency, you will choose to focus your attention on the present moment, the only moment that ever matters, and the gateway to your soul.

Your Conditioning Creates Disorder

If your mind is offered a choice between the spiritual journey and personhood, your mind will always choose personhood. The aspect of your life experience that is filtered by your mind is called *conditioning.* Your conditioning is the framework of how you see the world through the eyes of your mind-made self. Your conditioning is composed of a mixture of your perspective, judgments, beliefs, habits, religion, and culture, all of which keep you rooted in the world of form. Form is the dimension of what is perceivable with your eyes. There is a greater dimension known as the *formless,* in which divine intelligence is present in all that is unseen.

The present condition of humanity is largely unconscious. What you are aware of is your consciousness. What you are not aware of is your degree of unconsciousness. Unconsciousness is seen as complete identification with the conditioned mind. The good news here is that this lower evolutionary state is finally coming to an end. As a species, we are currently on the verge of a global shift into a higher state of consciousness. Thousands of people are waking up every day and realizing their inner dimension of peace and presence.

Our daily lives can be very challenging. The pace of maintaining our ego's position within our families and at the workplace requires our constant attention, and this results in stress. The burden of stress results in a decreased vibration and low energy responses to our challenges. When we react to our circumstances from the low altitude of our conditioned minds, our lives become even more problematic and dense. Our mind-made sense of self often seeks conflict in order to maintain its position of superiority and righteousness.

When people consistently choose to remain aligned with the dimension of form, they remain living subconsciously in fear of their inevitable death. It is our fears which make us accept our conditioning. Our minds are trained to accept fear. Again, through our mind training, we seek to escape fear by distracting ourselves with mindless absorption through television, mobile phones, movies, gaming, and sex. Sex is probably the greatest pleasure a human being can experience, but it is often used to escape reality. An insatiable craving for sensuality usually indicates the presence of internal poverty.

Choosing a more conscious life provides a great power that then allows you to be less distracted by the challenges of day-to-day life. A deeper understanding of your inner truth eliminates fear, lack, and limitation. What you practice becomes your consciousness. All trouble, anxiety, depression, and limitation are a result of your present level of unconsciousness. Before you are fully awakened, you shift back and forth for a while between consciousness and unconsciousness, between the state of pure presence and your state of mind. It takes time for deep consciousness becomes your predominant state. No patterns in your life can change unless you change your consciousness first.

The Unconditioning of Your Mind

In order to free yourself from your conditioned mind, you must first recognize your conditioning; then, and only then, can you detach from it. When people begin to align with that part of themselves that is eternal, they set themselves free in the dimension of the formless; it is from this altitude that we are able to ascend to higher planes of existence.

Identification with thought forms from your mind stream shifts your vibration out of alignment with your higher self. It is more favorable to keep your attention focused on the silent spaces between your thoughts and words. Consciousness is analogous to a large movie screen upon which all things come and go. You are the witness of all before you. We move toward order when we stop acting on only what is seen and align with the unseen aspect of ourselves. When you stay as the observing self, you can remain in a more expanded state of consciousness. This is because the self is the unbound and everlasting presence of your being. By remaining as the self, your mind and your conditioning can be observed and transcended.

For newly realized beings, it is important to have compassion for those still under the spell of their minds. This compassion should also always extend to ourselves. Compassion opens the door for a spiritual connection between souls, and it also opens space for spiritual healing and oneness to occur. In our awakening, we leave behind our mind-made identities, along with our need to judge everyone and everything. Judgment is the opposite of compassion, and it is also the default setting of the human mind. The goal of enlightenment is to activate your awareness and perception to a higher state beyond interpretation and labeling. When you remain as the witness of your experience, without judgment, you elevate your vibration and consciousness. Love and oneness are obscured by judgment. See more with your inner eye, and focus on looking at your world through the unfiltered lens of your soul.

Everything is consciousness, and every being is blessed with it. This empty space contains universal intelligence, which interacts with your body to initiate movement and function. This is where form and formless meet; this space is your center. *Space consciousness* is the awareness of this dimension in you. This inner vertical dimension is accessible to you through silence and stillness. An alignment with your formless self is available to you right now, and it is fully independent of the power of your mind.

Letting Go of Attachment

Let go of your attachment to people, places, and things. What weighs us down in the material world prevents us from moving about freely in the spiritual dimension. There is danger in wanting; wanting attracts more wanting. Want is the feeling of being incomplete. In order to dissolve attachment, want and need must merge. Do not become fixated on your situation. It is only a situation, another expression of form. Try to create space between you and your situation. No situation is impossible. Lighten your load so that you can soar at the altitude of mountaintops. This higher perspective on life is your hidden advantage. Let go of anything that no longer serves you, and free yourself. You cannot have attachment and freedom at the same time.

The Power of Surrender

Awareness is the unconditional surrender to "what is." By removing any resistance to the moment and by saying yes to what is happening in it, we find freedom. Surrender is the bridge between your resistance and nonresistance. Use the bridge to cross over into your divine stream of consciousness. Surrender allows you to let go of whatever resistance you are attached to, and to flow as you go. Because of the presence of fear, it can be difficult to turn over control of your life. What you are holding on to is stopping your surrender. Trust is the key to the process of surrender" Exchange your fear for faith, and give your life permission to expand. Know that what is available to you is a greater consciousness. Surrender to what is, and keep surrendering until there is nothing left to surrender to. Be at ease. Surrender is a doorway to inner peace, serenity, and liberation. If you continue to seek the peace of inner stillness, you shall find the presence of God.

Ten Steps to Surrender

1. Imagine a stress-free life, one that is free of tension. See yourself as a master of surrender to whatever moment, happy or sad, that life brings to you.

2. Believe in the transformative power of surrender. Faith is the fuel of success. Set a goal to become a lighter version of yourself every day.

3. Let go of your attachments. Attachment is the cause of human suffering, which breeds sorrow and discontent.

4. Quiet your mind and find stillness. In order to study yourself, thought-emotion must slow down. By placing yourself in the mode of observation without judgment, you will begin to see and understand yourself with clarity.

5. Rejoice in the hidden moments of happiness in your day. Make it a point to surrender to joy as often as possible.

6. Try to remain neutral to the events you see. Your conditioning compels you to always act or do something. You need not react to everything and everyone.

7. Be introspective; take a look at yourself as the witness of your experience. When you, the observer, are no longer being observed, your mind stream is transcended, and you are set free.

8. Embrace the power of change. Transformation is necessary to reach your next level reality. Don't fear change; welcome it. Fear constricts the expression of the self. Let go, and watch the dynamic transformative power of surrender act on your life.

9. Release expectations as to what your surrender will bring to your life. Allow the universe to deliver the people, experiences, and events that are in store for you. Allow, allow some more, and keep opening yourself up to spiritual expansion.

10. Beyond the world of knowledge is the state of *knowing*. Know that as a result of your surrender, you are meeting each moment of your life from the highest position possible: the state of presence. Blessed are the ones who reside in the dimension of presence. Surrender to love, surrender to life, surrender to presence, and surrender to God.

Soar Like an Eagle

When eagles soar, it is very majestic and graceful. Witnessing the flight of an eagle is pure bliss. Their initial flight is very challenging, with lots of energy used to flap their wings and navigate head-on air streams. Then, in one swift moment, a transition occurs: the wings suddenly become motionless, and the eagle appears to levitate as it begins to soar effortlessly. From afar, it appears as if the eagle finds a tailwind of momentum to sustain its flight. It becomes one with the wind, one with nature, and one with the universe.

Soaring is not just for eagles; we, as human beings, can also soar. In the atmosphere of the greater you, a less dense, lighter version of you is revealed. This aspect of you is the part of you that emanates your soul. This watchful and wise space is known as *presence*. Grace is the blessing that is bestowed on those who reside in the realm of presence. The realm of presence is effortless and free. In presence you are unlimited, and your being can soar to unimaginable heights. At the altitude of the greater you, there is no inner resistance; this inner calm enables you to remain completely present in the now, with little to no effort at all.

The Power of Yes

Your ego creates the resistance in your life. This is precisely what is saying no to life. Surrender is the shift from saying no, to saying yes to life. When you say yes to life, you are allowing life to flow through you instead of happening to you. This action of accepting and allowance is a portal to enter the vertical dimension of presence.

Don't argue with what is happening in your reality. When you are resistant to life, it is called *suffering*. All suffering is because you are believing that you have lost something. When you stand in opposition to what is happening in the present moment, you create more inner resistance. Expand your consciousness by saying yes to the present moment. Say yes to your experience. Say yes to what is. Saying yes to life is liberating. Free yourself from all internal resistance by saying yes to what the universe brings you.

Below are active properties of the word yes:
- The word yes is energized; it literally is positively charged and activates the law of attraction to support your vision. Saying yes puts your positive energy in motion.
- Saying yes invites new experiences into your life and promotes growth. Opportunities in life are few and far between. Say yes to getting more out of life; the word no tends to close doors and opportunities.
- Saying yes acts to eliminate your fears. The word yes creates space for success in your life. Yes instills confidence and purpose. Simply tell yourself, "I can do this."
- Saying yes activates the start of a new journey. What's new is what is available to you in the present moment. Say yes to this moment, this day, this opportunity, and this life.
- Yes triggers innovation and collaboration. Creativity is enhanced by the opportunity for expression. Yes invites other people to join your movement. Collaboration forms collective realities for each participant and strengthens oneness by linking individuals through a common purpose.

Conscious Manifesto

(Say aloud)
I trust the universe to bring me
the moments my soul needs to evolve.
I surrender to what is happening for me
right now and let go of all my resistance.
I believe that love is the highest power.
Love is the answer to all life's questions.
My path is the one of least resistance.
My mission is oneness: in myself, mankind,
and with the Creator of all there is.

My inner light of divine energy is my soul.
My soul's direction is always home;
energy always returns to its Source.
My home is one with God.

Everything Is Within

Everything is within.
Everything you will ever need is already inside your soul.
There is nothing in your life you can't become or accomplish.
You are both beautiful and limitless. There is no ceiling to your
capacity to learn or evolve. There is no world you can imagine
that is beyond your reach. Travel within to find the treasure of
your soul and the gift of surrender.

Your Soul Is Always There

Your soul is always there, right there by your side.
Listen for the whisper inside your silence; that is
the real you, the one and only you. You're not alone;
the universe lives inside you. There is only one love,
but there are many hearts. There is only one consciousness,
but there are many manifestations. You are only one soul,
but you alone can change the world.

Inside Each of Us Runs a Very Powerful River

Inside each of us runs a very powerful river of consciousness.
This roaring river runs deep inside your soul, a dynamic and
powerful stream of pure light consciousness that never runs dry.
It is a blessed force that serves you faithfully, and one that lights your way.
This inner essence is who you truly are. You are pure streaming intelligence
from the Source of the Most High. The current of your soul's river determines
your course in life. Don't try to be in control of your progression. You don't
need to know where you are going; simply be still in it. Let go of your
resistance and let your divine river run. Allow your journey to unfold
before you and flow as you go. Everything is happening as it should be,
when it should be, how it should be—and all is well.

You Are Not Your Mind

You are not your mind, because one day you will become forgetful.
You are not your sight, because one day your vision will fade.
You are not your hearing, because one day your hearing will dampen.
You are not your body, because one day it will fail.
You are the spirit underneath it all. The real you is the seer of
your thoughts, the magician behind your curtains,
and the light behind your loving eyes.

Free Yourself; Don't Resist

Free yourself; don't resist.
If you don't fully believe you can obtain what you aspire to,
this will show up as resistance in your life. Resistance is any thought,
belief, or action that stands in the way of what you desire.
No dream can manifest until you get into alignment with what you
desire. When you find peace of mind and let go of the expectations
of how your blessings need to happen, you create the proper space
for them to manifest. A universal alignment opens your
heart space to receive your blessings. An open heart isn't
afraid of breaking, and an open mind isn't afraid to learn.

The Moment You Realize

The moment you realize a certain behavior is causing you suffering,
this behavior has traveled from your subconscious mind to your conscious
mind. It is from this higher vantage point that you may choose to remove
this detrimental behavior to prevent it from presenting itself again. If you do
so, you will notice a boost in your consciousness. Conversely, if you fail to act
on this awareness, the same scenario, disguised as something new, will
present itself again—until you finally make the right choices and adjustments.
When we develop the skill to recognize aberrant, cyclical behavioral patterns
in ourselves, we feast on the gifts that recognition and awareness bring;
this step raises our vibration. When we embrace our divine truth, it
builds love in the heart and illuminates the beautiful gifts of the soul.

When Journeying Inward

When journeying inward, don't consider time and space parameters. On earth we are bound by the laws of time and space, but when we are connected to our souls, there is no limitation. Discovering who we really are begins with the path of self-awareness. As we journey inward, we will find inner peace and the keys to mastery over our physical reality. A conscious connection to our souls is always one purposeful breath away.

Go Beyond the Limits of Your Mind

Go beyond the limitations of your mind.
An untrained mind can be a source of suffering.
When your mind is quiet, you can experience
the awesome power of your soul rising.
At the soul level, there is no suffering,
only a state of being. Be present
in the here and now, but reside
at the level of your soul.

Pure Consciousness Is the Home of Your Flow

Inner stillness is the sanctuary of your soul.
When the mind is quiet, you enter a no-thought state. Once there, center yourself and just breathe. Time is of no consequence in the now, and your experience literally transitions into an elastic dimension of pure potential. Seek out and explore this flexible state of being. This is pure consciousness, your essence, and the home of your magnificent inner flow.

CHAPTER 5

Intention

Intention Is the God of Dreams

The power of intention is a great force in the universe, but most people don't know how to use it. If you can wrap your consciousness around the force of intention, you can bring dramatic positive changes to your life. *Merriam-Webster* defines *intention* as "an idea that one intends to do or bring about." The reason you need to master the power of intention is because of its intimate connection with manifestation. What you intend will always manifest in some form or another.

Purpose

Essentially, intention is purpose. What is the purpose behind your thoughts and actions of today? It is important to state your purpose because the more you practice your aim, the more divine momentum is added by the law of attraction, which brings the right circumstances, people, and events to manifest what you desire. An intention to have fun will usually bring it; an intention for clarity will also bring it. Failing to create daily intentions is like hopping aboard a train to nowhere. A train to nowhere goes nowhere. It is more favorable to direct your experience because your input determines your output. What you put in is what you get back. Your output is your level of productivity in life. You will become a more productive person when you hold true to your intentions. If you design a plan and a purpose each day, you can accomplish great things in a short period of time. Creativity is your divine gift, and your visions guide your creative direction.

You Are the Cocreator of Your Experience

Life has an infinite combination of experiences to offer. We are constantly sifting through life, making choices that determine our direction. We are consciously and unconsciously choosing the thoughts and ideas we want. If you remain asleep to the concept of being the cocreator of your experience, you are functioning as a receiver instead of the director of your reality. As human beings, we create our experiences through the choices we make, but we become the directors of our reality when we assume responsibility for our decisions, actions, and outcomes. To become a great director, you must see the big picture, make good choices, and make deliberate conscious movements that fill the spaces of your existence and complete your vision of yourself.

You can become a more efficient cocreator of your experience by practicing. Practice is the repetition of a behavior until it becomes part of your consciousness or routine. The more you practice the power of intention, the better you get at manifesting. Practice your intentions daily; speak them into existence. If you need to, write them down or post notes on your mirror at home. A good suggestion is to start a life journal or diary in which you write down your goals and innermost feelings. When you write things down, this process translates your thoughts and ideas into existence. However you choose to practice your intentions, do so frequently throughout each day. The universe is always listening, supporting, and responding to you.

The Meaning of Life

What is the meaning of life? Life has no inherent meaning everyone can agree on. Life is what you make of it. Each of us assigns a meaning to life and brings that belief into reality. When you identify your greater purpose and set the intention to achieve it, you begin to live life meaningfully. Most people live for the day or perhaps for the moment. When you live to extract meaning out of each of your experiences, every day becomes a blessing, and your existence becomes a powerful presence. I can imagine a world in which each being is able to realize their divine purpose and express what is true in their heart. The realization and expression of our truth adds meaning to our lives. Each of us travels the earth, searching outside ourselves for our hidden truth, when the secret of our divine gift is hidden where it has always been: in our hearts.

Set Your Intentions Toward Love

Set your intentions toward love.
Love is the strongest emotion in all existence, and it can be
used to navigate yourself out of any unfavorable situation.
When hardship and storms occur in your life, your outcomes
will depend on your willpower and resolve. The storms
themselves may be beyond your control, but you can always
choose your reaction to your circumstances. Love is always
one choice away. Fear is man-made; only love is real.

You Are Deserving of All Your Dreams

Many things we do are not in our best interest, but
we do them anyway. We act in regrettable ways because of our
broken hearts. Old habits die hard. If we truly want to be free,
we must allow part of us to die to save our souls.
Our aching hearts can be repaired, but the things we have
already done to others and ourselves can never be undone.
Don't believe that part of you that says you don't deserve this
or you don't deserve that. You deserve all your dreams.
Complacency leads to lack. Lack is a mind poison that distorts your
perception of the truth. You must continue to develop your mind,
body, and soul—or risk being outperformed by
an ever-evolving society.

It Is Your Will That Determines Your Way

Every moment contains the potential for both happiness
and sadness, bitterness and grace, love and hate,
triumph and tragedy, acceptance or regret.
Moment by moment, decision by decision,
the power of choice is inherently yours.
It is your attitude that creates your disposition,
and it is your will that determines your way.

If You Believe in Infinite Possibilities

If you believe in infinite possibilities, then commit to trying new things. New experiences expand our awareness and teach us the value of experiences over things. We can learn only what we don't already know. When we travel outside our comfort zone, we learn how to adapt to our discomfort, thereby enhancing our survival skills. Be spontaneous and joyful when possible. Joy is the emotion we feel when we are truly living in the moment. Live forward and don't look back. Don't let yesterday's news give you the blues. Your thoughts and experiences of today shape your circumstances and your world of tomorrow.

Each Day the Sun Rises, You Are Renewed

Yesterday cannot continue to exist without your permission. When you pass certain milestones in your life, celebrate your successes and forget your failures. A guilty mind experiences no pleasure. Let the past stay in the past. Each day the sun rises, you are renewed. Live in present-moment awareness and focus on vibrating at the frequency of happiness. Set your intentions toward abundance, and joy will find its way back into your life.

Points of Attraction

The role of intention setting and dream building is vital in your daily life. The visualization process creates the focus and trajectory of your path. If you lose your inspiration to set goals, you will undoubtedly suffer stagnation. By setting intentions for yourself, you establish points of attraction for the universe to act on and deliver all that you are asking for.

This Isn't a Cruel World

This isn't a cruel world; this is a loving world.
Once we align ourselves with this belief, we can come into alignment
with love's magnificent vibration and flow. When we begin to act
with love as our sole intention, we position ourselves to see love
in all things and all beings. Open your heart and prepare yourself
to receive what you desire. You are both worthy and deserving of
all your dreams. Know that the universe always supports you and
will attract the people and circumstances you need in order to evolve.
Your visions are like oxygen for the mind, body, and soul.
Maintain faith in your unique journey and behave as if your
desires have already been delivered. When you act with
love in mind, the universe will respond by sending you
an abundance of love and kindness in return.

The Velocity of Life

Sometimes we feel like we are stuck in the mud.
The velocity of our lives surely depends on our
intentions and the level of effort we generate to
propel ourselves toward love and light.
Nothing in life happens by itself.
It takes a magician to perform magic,
it takes a conductor to direct an orchestra,
and it takes deliberate, purposeful intentions to
speed your progression toward the greater you.

If You Can Dream It, You Can Attract It

Our dreams are what inspire us. Dreams are essential because
they create the focus and inspiration that drive our very existence.
A magnificent vision preceded each great accomplishment in your life.
To get free of your current situation, you must climb a ladder to
see things from a higher perspective. Each vision is a rung on the
ladder to your happiness and success. No situation ever changed
without a well-executed plan. You can change the momentum of your
life today by vividly visualizing your dreams and drawing them into existence.
Impossible is only a word.

CHAPTER 6

Manifestation

The Science of Manifestation

Perhaps God's greatest gift to mankind is the ability to create things from thoughts. Everything that can be seen in this world, from tall buildings to your iPhone, was created from a small thought or idea. Thoughts manifest things and create the conditions that allow your dreams to manifest. You are always manifesting something, whether you realize it or not.

Alignment with Your Higher Self

You create a better life for yourself when you are aware that your soul is always guiding you in the right direction. Your higher self knows what to do, how to do it, where you are supposed to be, who you are supposed to meet, and where you are going. The closer you are aligned with your higher self, the more powerful you become at cocreating your reality.

You are always connected to your higher self, but once you are born, a period of amnesia ensues, and all you have left is an ethereal connection. Despite these circumstances, it is possible to consciously and purposefully reconnect with your higher self and thereby initiate your manifestations from a higher perspective. The more you invite and call on your higher self, the more you strengthen the connection, and the more spontaneous and effortless your manifestations will become. Available ways to connect with your soul include residing in solitude and stillness, being in the now, meditating, being mindful, and having an inner dialogue with yourself.

Dreams

Another way to connect with your higher self is through your dreams. Our dreams connect us to the spirit world and higher consciousness. Everybody has dreams, but, unfortunately, not many people remember them. Your dreams don't arrive by accident. It is important to remember your dreams because they have symbolic messages, road signs, and answers to your questions encoded inside them. Every dream contains images and visions that can change and transform your life. Carl Jung, the father of psychoanalysis, considered dreams to be manifestations of the human unconscious mind trying to communicate messages to the conscious mind.

Others believe dreams are one of several ways in which the Divine communicates with humans. The more often you reconnect with your higher self, the greater your ability becomes to remember your dreams. I recommend starting a dream diary to journal all your dreams. A written record creates space for you to analyze and interpret them at a later date. Keep a pen and notepad by your bed to write down your dreams. Record them as soon as you wake up, before the details fade from your memory; dreams tend to be fleeting.

Recording your dreams actually enhances your ability to remember more of them. Dream dictionaries exist to interpret various images, numbers, and colors that appear in your dreams. By taking a closer look at your dreams, you can begin to see recurring themes, characters, and events. Recognizing dream patterns gives you greater insight into your soul. If you pay closer attention to more of your dreams, you gain access to the hidden power inside each of them, which you can then use to manifest your destiny and fulfill your higher purpose.

The Creative Process

Manifestation is the process of creation. One of the keys to manifestation is initiating the creative process when you are in a joyful state of mind. Joy acts as a point of attraction that allows you to deliver spontaneous joyful manifestations. When you can sustain your joy for prolonged periods of time, you are able to manifest effortlessly and also in bundles. For example, when you are in love, you are both joyful and, consequently, extremely productive.

When I first met my wife, Olivia, I found myself in a continuous vibratory bliss. As much as I want to claim that this next-level energy was a result of my own evolution, I cannot dispute that my days were brighter because of her presence in my life. I became a better son, father, man, and physician because of love. Since the arrival of my true love, manifesting has become easier because it now takes off from a higher energy state. When you are in love, you experience a high sense of harmony and wellness, which are the perfect conditions for manifestation to take place.

When you are suffering from sadness, this lack consciousness manifests as scarcity in your outer world. Your thoughts and emotions strongly predict the quality of your manifestation into your material world. "The only reason that something you want is not coming to you, is that you are holding yourself in vibrational harmony with something other than what you want," Abraham Hicks wrote. Your life is always coming together. Don't believe that what is happening to you, is not for you. Your life is never not unfolding.

Harmony

When you are in harmony with your powerful inner flow and in universal alignment, your ability to manifest is amplified. Try to minimize complaining, which only slows down the speed of your manifestations. Don't see the challenges inherent in your project as problems; see them as stepping-stones in the evolution of your plan. You will find the solutions you are looking for when you reside in your home frequency. Any inner resistance of yours is a measurement of your distance from Source. If you find yourself stuck, get unstuck by staying grounded and grateful in the present moment. The now is when life itself can be observed through a wider lens than just your two eyes. Take time to relax, reflect, and rejuvenate yourself. A rested mind and body are capable of creating amazing things.

Visualization

Along my journey, I have learned to use two powerful methods of manifestation: *visualization* and *visioning*. These are two distinct intellectual concepts. The first method is the practice of visualization. Dr. Ernest Holmes, the author of *The Science of Mind,* published in 1926, stated, "The first thing to do is to decide what you wish to image into the mind. Begin to see the complete outcome of your desires in mental pictures." One reason certain people fail to reach their visions is that they are unable to narrow their focus to illuminate exactly what they desire to accomplish. The greater the details of your visions, the higher the success rate of your manifestations.

The second step of visualization is to turn on all your five senses in order to see, hear, touch, smell, and feel the object of your desire.

The more detailed you can imagine your vision, the closer it comes to you. If you can do so, draw illustrations of your plans for your vision and create three-dimensional models of your ideas. When possible, speak about your dreams to whomever will listen. Seek support from your friends and contacts to aid in your dream's arrival. Spend your free time revising your plans and making them better. What you give your attention to grows.

The third step of visualization is picturing the vision as if it has already taken place. Experience how it feels to live the vision you desire. Imagine yourself as having finished your project, and see yourself reaping the benefits of long hours, dedication, and hard work. Visualize your project working for you and for the benefit of others. When your dream enhances other people's lives, it is likely to attract more momentum from the universe. Being unselfish is often rewarded with riches beyond money, fame, and power.

The final step of the visualization process is detaching from the outcome and allowing divine momentum to carry your dream forward. Don't get stuck in trying to figure out how everything must happen for you. Trust that the universe has already provided the perfect conditions for its manifestations. This opens your consciousness to being a receiver so that the desired outcome can come directly to you. When you place your trust in the greatness of the Divine, synchronicities beyond your imagination will start to appear.

Visioning

A higher method of manifestation is called visioning. The visioning process is the evolution, or deepening, of teachings Dr. Ernest Holmes originally put forth in *The Science of Mind*. Visioning is a concept based on the idea that we make ourselves available to what God is already doing in our lives, thereby catching what is already happening. Dr. Michael Beckwith, the founder and leader of the Agape Church in Los Angeles, is a well-known pioneer of visioning.

The key premise of visioning is that all divine ideas God has are within us already. "We tap into God's vision for our lives and ask ourselves the question, 'What is it that I have to become for that vision to manifest?' Visioning is always for self-transformation," Dr. Beckwith says. The vision is already accomplished in the mind of God. What we need to pray for is to be a willing and able vehicle for its accomplishment. According to Dr. Beckwith, "We become a living embodiment of God's ideas if we let God work through us. God is Divine Love revealing itself. As expressions of love, it is not surprising that the power of manifestation is at its greatest when we are operating from the high frequency states of love and joy."

Deliberate Creation

The action of manifestation is always in play, but the power multiplies when you become consciously aware of its presence and begin to use it intentionally. This is known as *deliberate creation*. In deliberate creation, one creates unconsciously less often and more frequently with conscious intent. When your actions are deliberate, they are powered by intention and filled with meaning and purpose. As a result, the universe responds accordingly by delivering your visions faster and with greater specificity.

Your skill level of manifestation is proportional to your level of spiritual consciousness. The deeper your awareness is, the more your intentions are born from visions of love, joy, and unselfishness. Mastering the art of manifestation requires you to remember your dreams. When you dream a dream you can remember, you can bring these visions into your awakened state, where you can use them and act on them. By doing so, you can change the trajectory of your life and live your dreams while you are awake. At its core, manifesting is easy. You do it every second of every day. You manifest instantaneously and effortlessly. You are great at it. The question is not, can you manifest? The question is, what are you manifesting?

Your Future Is Unscripted

Your future is unscripted;
you are rewriting it every single moment.
Each decision you make influences the next
moment, which in turn pushes your very evolution.
There are no limitations to the trajectory of your life;
you can go as far as your imagination carries you.
The only restrictions you have are the ones you are
currently placing on yourself. Visualize your desired
future often and focus your attention on your goals.
This activates the inner power of manifestation. There is
nothing you can't accomplish with focused intention.
Your greatest moment is at hand; now is the time to step
into your light. This is your moment of clarity.
The entire world is awaiting the greater you.

Great Things Can Happen for You

Great things can happen for you in life, but in order for
them to manifest, you must create and maintain the proper
thought space for your dreams to come true. We must always
hold close and dear the faith that everything is possible for us
in this lifetime. It is important to imagine your life in the future.
Every time you do this, you create an invisible thread that
stretches across space and time. Dreams establish virtual links
to your future self. All you have to do is follow the thread;
your desired event will soon follow.

Momentum

When you have a strong desire, it also carries
a powerful momentum capable of carrying you
all the way to your desired destination. Don't worry about
the how or when it will happen; focus on your strongest desire,
and your path will appear at your feet.

The Reason You Aren't Accelerating

The reason you aren't accelerating fast enough is
that you are carrying too much baggage. Most people
are weighed down from carrying around their painful past.
They carry the stress of today and the worry of tomorrow.
Let it all go. You can't change the past; you must accept it.
No need to worry about the future; you can't control it.
When you live in the present moment, you can be weightless
and free. Freedom arrives when you let go of the
thoughts weighing you down and holding you back.

There Is So Much Available to You

There is so much available to you in this unlimited universe.
You can manifest untold miracles if you start to believe
in their existence. Once you can imagine the impossible,
it instantly becomes possible. Your mind is a dream factory that
never stops working. If you can dream it, then you can achieve it.

Yes Is the Most Powerful Word

Yes is the most powerful word in the English language.
It welcomes all blessings your way to blossom into your
colorful world. Your dreams are awaiting your blessing
to manifest. All you must do is say yes. When we, as
spiritual beings, open ourselves to positivity and light,
we usher in moments of splendor beyond comprehension.

Happiness Abounds in the Now

Happiness abounds in the now.
The joy of life is available to you at this very moment.
Close your eyes and picture a person in your life who
brings happiness to you. Now allow yourself to smile.
There it is! By changing your focus and attention to
thoughts of unconditional love, you bring instant harmony
and joy to your heart. Live to love. Love to live.

Manifesting Is Easy

Manifesting is easy;
you do it every second of every single day.
You manifest instantaneously and effortlessly;
you are great at it. The question is not, can you
learn how to manifest? The question is, what
are you manifesting? You have the power to
speak something into existence. Vocalize your
dreams, no matter how far-fetched they are.
Mind training is real. The only person who can
make all your dreams come true is you.

This Is a Manifestation

(Read aloud)
This is a manifestation.
What I see before me today was created from
a single thought turned into a belief.
With the same power that creates worlds, I will
change my fate of tomorrow and boldly walk into
the future, with courage, conviction, and certainty.

CHAPTER 7

Crisis

The Storms in Life Are Inevitable

In everyone's life, there is always an event or a series of events that threaten their very existence. These unfavorable scenarios often come in the form of unexpected storms. The first big wave of the storm overtakes many people; they are swept away and never seem to recover.

Sailing your ship successfully through a storm requires calmness, trust, skill, and determination. Many storms can be avoided by quick and creative thinking, but some storms in life are unavoidable, and you must navigate through them. An ancient African proverb says, "Smooth seas don't make skillful sailors." It is helpful to remember that storms don't last; there is always a calm that follows. In the presence of this calm, storm waters recede, giving you an opportunity for reflection and growth. Joel Osteen states, "There are some things you can only learn in a storm."

Faith

When there is a crisis in your life, you must face it with courage and faith. Trust that your storm is present for a reason and remember it will soon pass. Every storm has a beginning, a middle, and an inevitable end. Along the way, keep faith that you have the resolve to endure your situation and come out on the other side. The problems that you experience in life are merely tools that are carving you into the amazing being you are capable of becoming. How you respond to your hardships shapes your consciousness.

In the midst of your storm, you will be tempted to give up, but you must not listen to this voice. Listen instead to the voice of your higher self. The voice of the self is always positive and encouraging, and it would never suggest that you give up. The voice of your higher self is never loud; it is always a whisper. You are supremely gifted and highly favored. No situation is impossible. When you have and maintain faith in God, you create space for miracles to happen. Remember that miracles happen only to souls who believe in the existence of miracles. A miracle is an extraordinary event that the power of God causes. *Guide to the Scriptures* says, "Faith is necessary in order for miracles to be manifested."

For a miracle to happen for you, you must completely surrender to your circumstances. Only then can a divine force intervene on your behalf. Humility is the exact vibrational state of attraction that brings forth acceptance. Once you are a vibrational match to it, you become open to receiving the miraculous transmission from God. A human being's vulnerability is a sweet fragrance to the Divine. Mercy is the blessing that God shines on the meek. You are guided by an Infinite Power that loves you. You are, and have always been, God's child. No matter what situation you are facing today, don't give up. You are enough. You possess the power, insight, and fortitude to endure any challenge that comes your way. All you need to do is keep believing in yourself and keep the faith that you will overcome your steepest challenge.

Resilience

The nature of a storm is that it will come and then eventually pass. Storms are merely temporary changes in your surrounding conditions. In a crisis, you may not be able to change your circumstances, but you do have a choice in how you respond to them. It is always useful to maintain a Zen-like presence during your crisis. If you can remain cool, calm, and collected, wisdom and grace can find you. Resilience and transcendence are two of your hidden powers. Like the sun that continues to shine behind dark storm clouds, your inner light is always shining. You can endure any scenario you face by showing the courage and the willpower to endure and transcend your pain.

Everybody will eventually be tested. Life spares no one; greatness is the descendant of the storms that you survive. Your storms are a call for you to confront, adapt, and transcend your circumstances. As human beings, we must rely on our fortitude and conviction in the midst of situations that seek to exploit our weakness. In the presence of a storm, you must also maintain your composure. This single action of stability also inspires and strengthens the souls around you who witness your struggle. If you can handle your crisis honorably, you will inspire those around you to do the same. Acts of courage breed imitation by others.

My Health Crisis

In May 2015, I was close to finishing my first draft of *The Greater You*. All was well in my life, and I was feeling great balance and optimism in the core of my being. However, shortly after my annual health screening, I received notice that my prostate-specific antigen (PSA) level was elevated. At the suggestion of my urologist, I underwent a biopsy of my prostate gland the following week. The needle biopsy of my prostate was the most painful experience of my life.

After the procedure, I felt so vulnerable, violated, hurt, and afraid. As Olivia and I left the hospital, I broke down in tears. My tears weren't coming from my physical pain but from my fractured emotional state. I had vivid mental images and frequent premonitions that I indeed had cancer. Somewhere deep inside my center, my soul was preparing me for the worst. I knew that despite my unfortunate circumstances, I had to remain positive to receive the best possible outcome, so I quickly composed myself. From that moment forward, I tried to remain as optimistic as possible, but there was a knowing deep inside me that I couldn't avoid.

After a long weekend of anxiety and uncertainty, my physician called me on Monday afternoon and informed me that I had prostate cancer. I felt a wave of numbness travel throughout every cell of my body. I hung up the phone, sat in my car, and cried. I was devastated and in shock. I cried for myself, for my wife, and for my unrealized future. At that moment, I instinctively knew my life would never be the same again.

When I finally pulled myself together, I drove home and shared the news with Olivia. We cried together. I held her tightly and tried to reassure her that everything was going be all right. In that moment, I saw fear in her eyes that I had never seen before. In the days that followed, I became overwhelmed with deep sadness and grief. My feelings stemmed from a sense that I had lost my dreams and potential.

I remember that my suffering mind kept sending me thoughts of death and dying. Shortly afterward, a period of isolation and depression came over me. I became quite inconsolable in my dark mind, and I found comfort only in long embraces from my wife and kids. I felt sad, alone, and defeated. My mind was constantly flooded with thoughts of my disease; as a result, I lost my appetite for goal setting, dreaming, visioning, and manifesting. I felt deeply sorry for myself, and I couldn't stop thinking and grieving over my condition.

I took off work for a week to process my diagnosis and come to grips with my divided state of mind. I spent countless hours in deep meditation and prayer. The more I prayed, the less alone I felt, and the more empowered I became. Gradually, my mind stopped sending me negative thoughts. After a week of solitude and prayer, I emerged from my meditative state with a more positive attitude and a sense of knowing that everything would be all right. Smiles replaced my tears, and my mood was rejuvenated to reflect optimism, strength, and resolve. Deep in my heart, I was certain my cancer had come to remind me that I am not my body.

As time passed, I began to see my health crisis as a test of the theories contained in this manuscript. In a funny way, I saw myself as a human experiment on the journey of awakening. As the author of *The Greater You,* a book about transformation and freedom from the body-mind identity, I was being called on to put my own theories to the test. My peace of mind was at stake. I knew if I could transcend my fears of death and find my identity as the limitless self, I could more accurately testify and fully endorse the journey of self-realization. I realized that after seven years of researching and writing the book, it was all a prep course for this critical moment in my life.

The soul knows all, and my soul had been directing me all along. Knowing the task before me, I made the conscious decision to surrender my body-mind identity to my heart and soul. I took a giant leap of faith, and just like that, I was reborn. I fully surrendered to my situation and circumstances, which enabled my spiritual transformation to take place. All my fears were dissolved in my open heart's expansion. As a result, I found great comfort in remembering my true nature. I ceased to have my identity tied to personhood and began to live my life as the more powerful and infinite self. Reflecting now on my crisis, I realize my attachment to my identity as the body mind prevented me from being completely free as the soul.

The soul is unlimited, unbound, timeless, spaceless, birthless, and deathless. From this new perspective, I could discern that my identification with my thoughts, emotions, and memories was the primary source of all my limitations. By silencing my mind, I learned that I could transcend my conditioning and get back into alignment with my truth. Despair sometimes appears as though it is the truth. That is the deception of the mind and the temptation of your lower self—that part of you that you must let go. The self is the witness of all that is perceivable and is pure loving awareness. The self has no attachments and is empty of any thought, emotion, or intention. At the level of the soul, one finds a peaceful presence where freedom abounds, wisdom presides, and love rules.

Prior to my surgery, my soul shared insights and visions of a successful procedure and a full recovery. From that moment on, I placed full faith in the Creator that all was well. Because of my experience with cancer, I no longer allow my thoughts or situations to rule me. I prefer to focus my attention on the way I feel. I simply choose to be happy and then become a vibrational match to that desire. I am deeply thankful to all my family, friends, surgeons, and medical personnel who assisted me in my recovery; they are my angels.

As a cancer survivor, I no longer take life for granted. I see each new day as an opportunity to live louder and love deeper. I practice mindfulness by staying present while doing the simplest of things. I try to live in the moment and reside in silence whenever possible. I currently set at least three intentions every morning, and practice visualization and visioning until what I visualize and vision is delivered into my universe. I no longer walk by sight alone; I also walk by faith. My relationships with my wife, children, family, and friends have also been transformed and have never been better. I see them now through new eyes filled with love, gratitude, compassion, and understanding.

Lighten Up

If you are going through a crisis right now, use it as an opportunity to lighten up. A crisis is a calling to drop the heaviness of unnecessary baggage in your life and awaken to a better and lighter version of you. There are no coincidences in life. Many events that happen to you are actually road signs that point you to a different direction. Although the direction of your path may change, the goal remains the same. Home always represents going back to God.

Life is most certainly a gift and should be cherished every single moment. It is a fact that over one hundred fifty thousand people die in the world every single day. These people will never open their eyes again to see the magnificence of the sunrise or the serenity of the sunset. If we all could see life in the light of gratitude, there would be no time to argue or fight among ourselves. There would only be thankfulness for this moment, compassion for those in need, enough love to mend every broken heart, and ample understanding to end all global conflict.

The healing journey is a sacred space of calm, ease, serenity, and flow. To be healed is to be free of the contraction of the mind and to comfortably rest in the open space of heart consciousness. The state of wellness can always be found in the universal alignment of body, mind, heart, and soul. Peace is the place that exists in the harmony of oneness.

The Scars of Life Are Inevitable

The emotional scars of life are inevitable.
Deep wounds to the soul can set us back and hold us down.
We can avoid many painful experiences by making more conscious
choices in our lives. Despite all our precautions, there are some
painful experiences that cannot be circumvented; after all, life is
here to be experienced. Your path is yours and yours alone.
When a crisis arises, we must rise above our situation with courage
and grace. Faith is maintaining your beliefs when all hope has faded.

No Matter Where You Find Yourself Today

No matter where you find yourself today, there is a way forward.
No matter how hard your circumstances are or what you may
have done, there is a way through. Don't believe me because
I am saying so; believe it for yourself because there is a better way.
All good things start with a belief. A belief is merely a repetitive thought
that you invest in. Start building on a positive belief today, and tomorrow
that belief can become your reality. Your circumstances may be
challenging, but anything is possible if you just believe.

Emotional Healing

When you feel broken, remember that not everything is broken.
Cling to the angels who support you in this realm.
Feel and embrace the support of those who inspire you.
Slowly build yourself back up into a stronger, more durable spirit.
Your spirit is larger than any crisis coming your way.
We are all going to face moments of truth in our lives that
will shake our foundation. A crisis is merely a challenge
that serves to sharpen our resolve and willpower.
It is our will that determines our way.
Our way is forward, and the horizon is our trajectory.

When We Lose a Great Love

When we lose a great love, we feel hurt and sustain a significant amount of emotional damage. These wounds result in the formation of scar tissue around our hearts. If this tissue is allowed to harden, it can prevent us from ever accessing our vulnerability again. A frozen heart is not only cold but also frequently unforgiving. We believe we are protecting ourselves from ever suffering again, but what we are really doing is building walls made of nothing but excuses. This pain creates separation that can prevent us from ever falling in love again. Remember that being broken open also comes with the opportunity to be healed.

The Critical Moments in Your Life

The critical moments in your life can serve as an axis for your spiritual transformation. Adversity builds character and gives birth to self-analysis. Just because you have experienced a setback doesn't mean you can't bounce back. Within your skill set, you have the capacity to learn and adapt to any situation. Setbacks are temporary roadblocks, that's all. On the other side of your fiercest battle lies your greatest victory. When you are facing challenging circumstances, take advantage of the opportunity to pivot in a new direction. A new perspective allows you to see and respond to the world in a different way. Adjusting your viewpoint improves your vision and welcomes clarity where there was once doubt.

Remain Cool, Calm, and Collected

Don't let the stress of your job or situation throw you out of alignment. Keep calm during a crisis. Breathe consciously and know that in the end, everything will work out in your favor. Everyone faces storms in life that can be both unpredictable and frightening. When you allow an angry response to invade your body, your power is diminished, and your vibration is lowered. Don't allow your circumstances to manipulate your emotions. You aren't your situation. Always remain cool, calm, and collected before choosing your responses. If you can remember these three Cs, they will help protect your vibrational alignment.

Meet People Where They Are

Meet people where they are and don't try to move them.
Allow them to fully experience their crisis. Crisis is a
vector for a change and transformation. Respect their
experience by being supportive and compassionate.
Don't judge them and don't pity them. Storms are
a call for souls to be more than they already are.
Allow those in crisis to respond to their challenges in the
best way they can. Resist your temptation to fix them
or their situation. If you want to assist their spiritual
breakthrough, then just listen and be present for them.
Encourage them, feel their hearts, and simply love them.

The Storms of Life

Everyone faces storms in their life. If you aren't currently facing a
crisis, then you are likely unaware of the one looming. Life is like
a thrilling roller-coaster ride. Between every two mountains is one valley.
After you accomplish one goal, another challenge will always appear.
Storms are an opportunity for personal growth and expansion of your
consciousness. The end rewards of your challenges are: learning life
lessons, mastery over your experience, spiritual transformation,
resilience, and the evolution of your soul.

When You Are Feeling Lost

When you are feeling lost, have an inner dialogue with your soul.
Your soul intuitively knows how any situation can and will work out.
The physical mind sees from the perspective of a valley, whereas
the soul sees things from the perspective of a mountaintop.
If your higher mind is left out of your thoughts and decisions,
you cannot generate your absolute best effort. Conversely, when
the higher mind is activated, you are engaging your soul's wisdom.
When you follow your soul, the resultant energy will generate your
most favorable outcomes. The higher mind is the voice of your soul.

CHAPTER 8

Resistance

Flow and the Path of Least Resistance

In the sport of sailing, resistance is often described as the wind against a boat's sails. The wind slows the boat's speed and prevents rapid acceleration. In life, it is common for people to project resistance onto an angry partner, a difficult boss, or a child who doesn't listen well. All resistance outside ourselves is defined as external resistance. However, our greatest enemies in life, combined, account for only a small fraction of our total resistance. Our greatest obstruction is internal resistance. A combination of painful memories, self-doubt, poor self-respect, anger issues, victim mentality, and anxiety all represent aspects of ourselves that hold us back. Sometimes we see life as a problem. As long as we view life as a problem, we will continue to look for the answers to life. Life is not a problem; it is an experience. If we can begin to see ourselves as life itself, then there will be fewer problems and far fewer questions to answer.

Be Free Where You Are

This chapter addresses resistance: the external and internal forces that prevent you from finding and experiencing the dimension of the greater you. Your approach to the resistance in your life is the key to finding your way to a more peaceful existence. Resistance lowers your energy and decreases your vibration. People often speak of being stuck. Getting stuck is about holding on too tightly. It's easy to get anchored, holding on too hard to a thought, relationship, or belief. Releasing resistance is the process of letting go of our attachments. Surrendering to the path of least resistance is the key to increasing your inner power. Ultimately, when you die and leave your physical body, there is no pain, struggle, or resistance. But why wait until then to enjoy the freedom of letting go? You can be free where you are today. Letting go of your inner resistance and mastering your encounters with outer resistance will allow you to experience freedom and peace in the here and now.

If you are looking for the path of least resistance in your life, it is right where it has been your whole life: at your feet. My personal aha moment was when I realized the path of least resistance was a way to connect with my higher self. I started to comprehend and exercise the power of surrender. I began to allow my experiences to unfold for me instead of always trying to direct my experience. I ceased to believe that life needed to be a struggle about this or that. I stopped thinking I needed to win a fight with someone in order to taste the feeling of victory. I began to see my life as a rhythmic sequence of teachable moments. I started this journey looking for victories, but I ended up finding my inner peace.

Childhood Pain

Too much of our pain as human beings has its origin in our childhood and is buried deep in our past. Additionally, many people experience stress and anxiety worrying about their uncertain future. Some people never stop worrying. Stress contributes to mental fatigue and disease. Stress is the result of trying to anticipate the future. For us to live more abundantly, we need to focus on living in the now. There is nothing wrong with this moment. What is available to us right now is universal love. If we can open our hearts to access our deepest emotions, our feelings can be used as a guidance system to deliver us into our brightest possible outcomes. Stop believing you are a prisoner of your past. Stop worrying about a future you don't control. Immerse yourself in the present moment and live love now.

I spent my entire childhood and young adulthood building walls to protect myself against the outer world. I built these walls under the loving direction of my parents and extended family. I was instructed not to talk to strangers, and I was advised to guard myself against the outside world. My family taught me these principles to help me stay safe and prevent me from being hurt. While it is true that we need this layer of protection as children, the opposite is true for walking a spiritual path. As a conscious man, I came to the realization that I had to tear down the very same walls that had once isolated and protected me. I simply learned to trust my own unique journey. My old beliefs were replaced by new ones, which made way for exponential growth and change.

Now I can trust the same world I was taught to fear. Spiritual transformation requires the removal of your outer shell to reveal the brilliance of your inner light. You must learn to recognize the displays of your lower mind when it is in the resistance mode. Fear, anxiety, confusion, and anger all represent emotions of resistance. Make it a habit to monitor your mental and emotional state throughout each day. Have a look inside yourself and ask, *What is going on inside me?* Each negative thought reflects your resistance to the present moment. All fears arise when you live from the identity of your body mind and reflect a failure to find your presence. When you connect with your inner presence, all fears dissolve. Love is all there is in the now, and fear cannot exist in the presence of love.

Victim Mentality and Blame

Many people are aware of the benefits of living in the moment, but they unconsciously continue to display their fears and anxiety at every possible opportunity. This is an example of broken consciousness. When we fail to embrace our higher self, we do so because it is more comfortable to fail than to succeed. In failure, we receive the attention and compassion the ego craves, allowing us not to take responsibility for our circumstances. This is an example of a victim mentality. Indeed, some people never stop worrying and shifting blame for their misfortunes. The way to get out of victim mentality is to acknowledge your fears, own them, let them go, and move on. Fear and doubt are constant companions: fear produces doubt, and doubt produces fear. The power of faith erases both fear and doubt. Faith is an energy within you; it isn't a belief. It is knowing that all is well and that you are a loving reflection of the Divine. "Faith is the oil that gets the friction out of living," Les Brown once said. Replace your fear with faith, and change your world.

The Moment of Fear

Twenty years ago, I had the experience of white-water rafting in the Balinese jungle. The excursion started high in the mountains of Ubud and ended with me jumping out of the canoe into the Ayung River, in nothing but my life vest. Initially, because of my fears, I was reluctant to jump into the roaring river, but at the critical moment of my journey, that is exactly what I did. Casting hesitation aside, I trusted my instincts and jumped into the river.

As I floated swiftly downstream, I was advised to let go and not resist the current of the river.

As I floated farther downstream, I had a spiritual revelation. The river knew exactly where it was going, and as long as I didn't resist, I became part of it. I trusted that it knew where it was going and that it would carry me to safety. This journey opened my eyes to the power of letting go. Just like the river, there is a very powerful stream of energy that flows in all beings. I learned to trust that I am always right where I need to be, and with that trust, I learned to let go of the need to always remain in control.

All fear is psychological. The voice of fear or faith—these are your choices. You can give your attention to your inner critic, or you can follow the whisper of your higher mind. Whichever one you choose will determine everything else in your life. Fear and happiness constantly battle for your attention. You need to make a choice, so choose the joy available in the present moment.

Let go of fear and doubt, and trust your journey. You are here to be joyful and to evolve. If impedance is already present in your life, then find a way to release it and let it pass through; this is the way of ease. Liberation is possible if you leave your thoughts and limited beliefs behind and reside in the wave of the moment. In the now, you can be free of the limitations of who you are in the body mind. When you are in alignment with your wholeness as a nonphysical being, you can be free. What is standing in your way of a pure experience is what you are adding to it. This is your resistance; let it go. You will find the life you love when you are able to drop your resistance. What is left behind is your beautiful alignment with the greater you.

Self-Analysis Prevents Paralysis

You aren't stuck. Every morning, you have the opportunity
to imagine and create. If you are in a holding pattern,
then change is required. Self-analysis prevents paralysis.
Uncover, change, and evolve. Your path is always at your feet,
even when you don't see it. When you think you have lost your
way, you have only temporarily forgotten your purpose. It is time
to reset your target goals and allow yourself to dream again.
What if you died tomorrow? How would you live today? Follow your
intuition, follow your heart, and accelerate into the greater you.

Exchange Your Fear for Faith

Being fearless requires you to break free of past patterns that
have enslaved you. Fear keeps you away from your deserved glory.
If fear is your constant companion, then you must separate from its
viselike grip. The soul cannot experience fear; your soul is
made of pure love and light. The mind and ego create fear,
and the body then experiences it. Control the mind, and the body
will follow. Fear has cost millions of souls their dreams and provided
many more with the only excuse they have ever needed to fail.
Imagine your life if you could be unafraid.

The Shadow Self

The shadow self is that part of us that holds us back.
The shadow self resides in our subconscious mind and is
the holder of our fears. Managing this aspect of ourselves is
one of the most challenging and important tasks of our lives.
If you don't face this darker side of yourself, you won't be able
to fully absorb the loving light the universe is sending your way.
Let more love into your heart; love heals. Never lose faith in yourself,
and take the time to celebrate the vibration of your higher self.
Walking consciously down your spiritual path is the key to casting
light onto your shadow self and living in alignment with your soul.

An Extraordinary Way of Life

An extraordinary way of life is within your reach.
Your inner power lies in your alignment with your authentic self.
When you discover your buried truth, you set yourself free.
The fire of love that burns in your heart extinguishes any fear.
When fear disappears, freedom rings. Everyone has one thing
they are born for. Your signature frequency transmits a signal from
inside your loving center. Claim your divine blessing of inner
knowing, and the world shall know the awesome power of your gifts.

Your Greatest Weakness

Your fear of fully embracing your truth is your greatest weakness.
This is because aligning with your true self would leave you with no
more excuses for failure. This would end the era of blaming others
for your results. This ego shift would make you fully responsible for
your life. This is a powerful choice we all will face in our lives.
Shall I keep living as I am now, and hope for the best? Or do I choose
to unleash my inner gifts and see where my soul leads me? Choose
greatness and activate your awesome inner power. Embrace the ancient
knowing of your sacred inner being and unleash your divine greatness.
Accept the responsibility of your role as the cocreator of your reality.
You can accomplish anything and everything at the level of your soul.

When We Put Up Walls

When we put up walls to guard ourselves from becoming a victim or
being hurt, we believe those walls are actually protecting us.
In truth, we become prisoners behind those very same walls.
No one can climb over them, and we are trapped behind them.
Emotional hurt and resentment lead to loneliness and isolation.
The problem is that vulnerability and love are on the other side of these walls.
Abundance and happiness are on the other side of these walls.
Your potential cannot be reached behind your great walls. Tear down
your walls and free yourself from the prison of your own mind.

CHAPTER 9

Inspiration

Creating a Life You Love

No matter where you are in your life, keep moving forward. If you remain stagnant in your position, life will act on you instead of you acting on it. We must all hold close and dear that there is a force of good inside us that guides us and lights our way. If you believe in the presence of this power, you can activate it and reach your highest potential. The boundless glory awaiting you is cloaked by your history of attachment to safety. In order to win the gold, you must be able to turn potential into power and possibility into productivity.

Dream Big Dreams

Most people never reach their potential because they are content with playing it safe. If you want to be extraordinary in life, you must be aggressive and take some risks. Most people are dreamers who can experience their dreams only when they are asleep. Instead, your mission must be to live your dreams while you are awake. Make sure your dreams are big and bold. If you aren't dreaming big dreams, then you aren't really dreaming at all. To manifest your visions, you must speak them into existence. When you speak of your visions and share them with others, you open yourself up to receive assistance from the infinite intelligence of the universe. It is possible to use the frequency of the universe to increase your chances of a successful outcome. When you see yourself as an extension of the universe, this invitation allows the universe to act on your vision and activate the law of attraction to bring the right people, at the right time, to assist you.

Angels

All dreams need the support of dream builders—otherwise known as angels—who provide heavenly assistance along the way. Angels live among us and always appear in our lives when we most need them. God sends them to assist us, and they are often disguised as ordinary people. Angels form an invisible circle around us, which embraces, lifts, and puts us on the side of all that is good. Sometimes the support of an earth angel is the very thing in our lives that makes it possible for us to go on. Angels restore our faith in ourselves and reinforce the awesome presence of God.

As a human being, as long as you are trying and don't give up, there is hope and a bright future for you. God is undoubtedly always moving you forward. When you feel lost or broken, don't be afraid to seek help from others. The very person you turn to may be the angel you have been looking for. Stay open to the presence of angels in your life. With openness, you create the space for miracles to happen on your behalf.

Activate Your Dream

For your dreams to manifest, they must be pulled from your subconscious into your consciousness. In other words, you must move your dream from the intangible state of imagination to the tangible state of reality. This is how a dream activates into a action plan. Once a dream becomes activated, your mind can act on it in your awakened state. Visualize your idea as often as possible and see it in your mind as already done. Best results are achieved when you hold your vision in your consciousness every day.

Your action plan has a higher percentage of success if you see your project as a dance with life instead of a struggle. If working on your project doesn't add joy to your life, it probably isn't the right one for you. The mere mention of your project should bring a smile to your face, which affirms you are indeed pursuing your higher purpose. Keep a positive vibration in your core being. If you are positive and passionate about your plans, then other people will pick up on your energy and be inspired to be a part of your success. When something does go wrong—and it will—a positive attitude will give you power over your circumstances, instead of your circumstances having power over you. Life isn't a straight path; it is a spiral with many unexpected twists and turns. Try to see your setbacks as opportunities to pivot and grow in a different direction. Your dedication and persistence go a long way. Every vision has a natural flow or vibration to it. Become a vibrational match to the energy of your dream, and, like a plant, it will grow exponentially. Be a caretaker of the soil of your project, nourish it with attention and love, and it cannot help but expand.

Positivity

Nothing can stop a driven person with a positive attitude from reaching their goal. Positivity creates a magnetic environment that attracts positive people and positive results. Despite your optimism, there will be doubters who attempt to push you off your course. Some people feel it's their job to crush other people's dreams and confidence. Be sure to avoid those individuals who seek to diminish your energy and discourage you. There has never been and never will be a shortage of energy vampires. Some people use energy as a tradable commodity. "Let me take from others because I feel depleted" is their motto. Never let the negativity of detractors rub off on you. Many times, some people are unable to accept your transformation because they feel powerless to change themselves. Positivity is the seed of productivity. It helps to always see yourself as growing and evolving toward the greater you. Be relentless in the pursuit of your dreams. Simply be unstoppable. Always give one hundred percent effort; don't hold back, and never quit on yourself. It's all or nothing at all.

Fear Is a Dream Killer

The things that stop most people in life are self-doubt and fear itself. Fear is a dream killer and ends more people's dreams than can ever be counted. Most people in this world die without ever reaching their potential. When they die, their dreams go to the grave with them. Everyone has a higher purpose buried deep in their consciousness. By finding your true self and remaining as presence, you can reach your untapped potential. Your joy is a treasure map to your higher purpose. Once you discover your signature purpose, pursue it with all the passion and enthusiasm in your heart. A universal alignment with your mind, body, heart, and soul activates your highest life trajectory. From the position of alignment with your pure self, you can vibrate at your signature frequency and deliver your signature gift.

To accomplish great things, you must be courageous and highly motivated. Perhaps your motivation comes from a deep desire to change your circumstances, or perhaps you have a desire to provide financial stability for your parents or your children. It all starts and ends with you. You are the captain of your ship, and you must sail your vessel through every storm with certainty, conviction, and clarity.

Work Your Plan

Work on your vision for at least thirty minutes a day. Make changes when necessary, and it will begin to take form. The creative process is the transformation of an idea from a thought wave to a particle, the very essence of manifestation. Your odds of a successful project vastly improve if you do extensive research before launching it. Many ideas and businesses have failed because of poor timing to market. Timing is everything. If you discover that your idea is already taken, perhaps you can make a better version of it. Consult entrepreneurs whom you admire and adopt those of their habits that work for you. If possible, find a mentor for your project. We all need mentors and motivators in our lives. If you can't find a mentor, you can improve your skills by watching inspirational videos or reading books on the subject. Leave no stone unturned. Increase your mind power by adding to your current skill set and remain open to adding partners to your action plan.

Share Your Dream

When I was writing *The Greater You,* I relied on the expertise of many successful people who were already in my life. This is how the practice of sharing your dream can create momentum. Sharing your vision inspires others and facilitates a synchronicity and powerful creative force that cannot be stopped. Share your dream with those close to you. You can elevate the consciousness of your entire soul group. To be successful, you must maintain a creative mind-set and have the desire to get more out of life than you are already getting. Never be complacent; complacency is a precursor for failure. Pursue your excellence daily with all the ability that you can possibly access.

You Are Unlimited

If you are medically ill or disabled, or have been severely affected by a chronic illness, don't let your medical diagnosis be the source of limitation in your life. You are not the body mind; you are a highly charged unlimited spirit. Your soul is a light inside you that radiates outward toward the heavens. Be mindful not to see yourself as limited as a result of your handicap. In my own case, when I was diagnosed with cancer, I temporarily stopped dreaming. I was so preoccupied and consumed with negative thoughts of doom and gloom that there was no mind space left for any light to shine through. No matter how hard I tried, I couldn't remember any of my dreams. If you stop dreaming, you become susceptible to stress, anxiety, insomnia, and depression. When you dream, it is confirmation that you are alive and well. Dream often and dream big. Like the universe, your potential is infinite. Bringing your dreams to life is proof of your divine connection to Source and the effectiveness of your antenna as a receiver for the mind of God.

My health crisis led me to question many things about myself, including the trajectory of my life path. I turned inward to my center, and I started an inquiry within. I benefited from self-analysis. When clarity finally arrived for me, I felt stronger and more focused than ever. I was strengthened by the belief that I wasn't finished yet, and I felt reenergized. Virtually overnight, I was projected into a more grateful and productive existence. I became supremely motivated to see my dream project *The Greater You* come to fruition. My faith was magnified by the belief that there was nothing that could stop me from evolving into light.

As my depression lifted, I became more connected to the beauty of nature that surrounded me. Once again, I began to notice the cycles of the sun and moon. I began to hear the birds sing again in the morning, and I looked forward to hearing the crickets and owls at night. The simple things in life reinvigorated me, and, eventually, I began to smile again. When I did smile, I noticed that the more I smiled, the more people smiled back at me in return. A short time later, my nightly dreams returned to me, and, once again, I began dreaming dreams that I could remember.

The Gift of Life

Another important factor needed to reach your full potential is to become a seeker of your inner truth. Everyone has a higher purpose in life, but very few people answer the call of self-realization. Many people live their lives behind a veil of excuses, buts, and what-ifs. These individuals often live in regret, with their potential largely unfulfilled. The present moment offers the opportunity and space for everyone to live their dreams right now. It's a mistake to wait for the perfect conditions to pursue your dreams, because life is inherently unpredictable. Tomorrow isn't promised to anyone. We all know someone who died prematurely and unexpectedly. Life is the ultimate gift, and it should never be taken for granted. When you harness the power of now and attach that incredible force to your vision, positive changes begin to happen. The law of attraction is activated, and divine momentum becomes your constant companion.

Success Is Built on Failure

Be bold and original with your ideas. If you aren't bold and ambitious, you risk being left behind in the fog of complacency. Dream a dream that you can remember. A dream that keeps revisiting you is called a vision. Visions are tightly linked to your higher purpose. The reason most people aren't successful at activating their dreams is because they are too afraid to fail. "Success is not built on success, it is built on failure. It is built on frustration and sometimes it is built on catastrophe," Sumner Redstone once said.

All successful people have had past failures in their lives, but they used them as learning opportunities to improve themselves and their formulas. The most famous example of this is Michael Jordan, the world's greatest basketball player. As a high school sophomore, Michael failed to make the varsity basketball team. His failure fueled his passion and competitive nature, which in turn motivated him to work harder than ever. Being cut from the team created in him an intense desire to succeed, and he used his disappointment as motivation to become the most decorated basketball player in the history of the game.

It's Up to You

The key to a successful life is to always give your best effort, not excuses. If you aim high enough and try hard enough, success will surely find you. People who are afraid to fail make constant excuses so that they never have to challenge or confront themselves. Everyone knows someone who is always making excuses in their life. Excuses serve people only as permission slips to fail. To achieve greatness, you must take ownership of your deficiencies and cast aside excuses. Recognizing your deficiencies is the only way to improve them. Make an honest list of your weaknesses, and then develop an action plan to turn your weaknesses into strengths. If you let doubt creep into your visions, you are finished. "If the Sun and Moon should ever doubt, they'd immediately go out," William Blake wrote. Practice seeing yourself successfully living your dream, and hold tightly to the belief that it is your divine destiny to deliver your higher purpose. If you are currently sitting on a dream, get up, get busy, and activate your vision. If you are willing to do the work, greatness is at hand.

You Are Capable Beyond Measure

The promise of a joyful existence is yours.
Along your journey, there will be those who try to slow you down,
but they won't succeed. No one but you can delay your spiritual
progression. When suffering does occur, treat it as an opportunity for
transformational healing to take place. Your gift is your soul, and your
divine light will always overcome any darkness sent your way.
No matter how long it takes, your wounded heart will ultimately be healed.
In your center is where you will find the greater you. Prove to yourself that
you are capable beyond measure, deeper than your circumstances require,
and giving beyond tomorrow's promise.

You Are Enough

You are enough.
You possess the one commodity that cannot be bought, sold, or traded.
You have a soul gifted from God and sent straight from heaven.
Dipped like a candle in blessed love and light, nothing but your fears
can stop you. Your inner strength and fortitude simply won't let you fail.
Even your circumstances don't matter; only your vibrational
alignment matters. Staying connected to Source energy
enables you to operate at your highest level.
You are blessed and destined to pass all the tests of time.
You are divine love itself, and you are indeed enough.

The Answer

I want to give you the tools to be free. At your very feet lie all answers.
The answer is always love—a love for yourself, for your neighbor,
and for your fellow man. The era of love is here.
But before you find your way, you must awaken from the illusion
that is your current reality. The key to everything is beyond your mind.
Behind the veil of life is the unseen, your truth. Freedom is on the
other side of your busy mind. In the land of no mind, there is a place for you.
If I told you there is a way to wisdom, joy, and fulfillment, would you be
willing to have a look? Good. Then have a look at the light of love.
When you follow love, all your questions will ultimately be answered.

The Purpose of Your Problems

The problems that you experience in life are
merely tools that are carving you into the most
amazing being you are capable of becoming.
How you respond to hardship shapes your consciousness.
The realization of your highest potential starts with an
epic shift away from your ego-based identity,
into a far greater soul-based identity.

You Are Not Average

You are not average; therefore, you are not supposed to be
living an average life, in which you unconsciously repeat negative
thought patterns. You are an extraordinary being created and
sustained by an unlimited power. You are simply amazing.
No matter what circumstances you are facing today,
set the intention in your mind to live an incredible life.
The only thing that can stop you from doing this is you.

Be Unstoppable

Be unstoppable.
Ultimately, it is about your ability to persevere in life.
Life happens to everyone along the way. Life is here to be experienced.
We will all face adversity in the times ahead. Your triumphs depend on
your willpower to overcome any challenging circumstances that get in
your way. Be courageous and reach deep inside your soul where
your inner power is unlimited. Keep striving to achieve your highest
dreams, despite any setbacks. No matter what happens to you,
never lose faith in yourself. We become who we believe we are.

Greatness Is a River That Flows in You

Your inner being is here to make a significant difference in the world.
This beautiful reality would not be the same without your very presence.
Greatness is the river that flows deep inside your soul. Be fearless because
you cannot drown. Your spirit is both buoyant and storm resistant. Only the
torrents of self-doubt that exist in the dark confines of your mind can destroy you.
It is your inner greatness that must emerge today to save your soul of tomorrow
Celebrate the divinity that resides within you and all of mankind.

On the Other Side of Impossibility

On the other side of impossibility is possibility.
There is no situation you cannot survive.
Faith is the torch you must carry throughout your dark nights.
Without faith, there is no light. If you truly believe in your inner power,
it can act on your behalf. Without faith, you are susceptible to the
external forces of the world. It is by faith that all things are possible,
and it is the key to your survival. Faith is the assurance of what we
all hope for and the conviction of things unseen.

Forgiveness Is Self-Love

Let the hurt stop and let the healing begin. It has been
far too long and much too hard on you. Allow today to be
a day of atonement. Let this moment signal a fresh start
and a renewed purpose. When we forgive ourselves and
those who have broken our hearts, we free ourselves from
any cognitive dissonance. If you follow your soul, it doesn't
allow you to block your blessings. What you resist persists.
Get out of your own way to allow the emergence of the greater you.
Without the presence of the resistance you are adding, your flow
is dramatically increased. Embrace the path of self-love in
the land of forgiveness. You are most deserving,
and you stand to gain so very much.

CHAPTER 10

Present-Moment Awareness

Mindfulness Matters

Mindful meditation brings your mind's attention to the present moment, without thinking about the past or the future. Mindfulness fine-tunes the mind into a relaxed state and gently brings you into the portal of the now. Mindfulness is simply focusing your attention on what you are doing in the moment, without attachment to anything. Any activity can be enhanced if you do it mindfully. For example, when you walk during the course of your day, you may do so mindfully. When you set the intention to walk mindfully, bring your attention to feeling the sensation of every step as each foot contacts the ground.

The Practice of Mindfulness

The planet earth contains the cosmic energy of roughly 4.5 billion years of existence. This electromagnetic energy is transferred from the center of the earth to you, through the soles of your feet. This is why so many wise souls walk barefoot. Be thankful for your ability to move about God's green earth freely. Take your strides with a sense of gratitude and purpose. Hold your head high, pull your shoulders back, and put a smile on your face. Similarly, everyone can drink water mindfully. Look at your glass of water with gratefulness for the journey the water had to take to arrive at your table and into your cup. Smile at the water and appreciate the nourishment it will provide to your body and mind. Drink your water slowly and sensually to experience its sacredness. Taste its freshness as it flows into your mouth and over your tongue. Be thankful for your ability to swallow, and receive the water with gratitude. Feel the increase in your satisfaction and energy levels.

In addition, everyone can eat mindfully. For example, take an apple. The apple has passed through many workers' hands to arrive on your plate. Give thanks to the tree that grew the apple and to the farmers, pickers, and merchants who brought it to the market for you to buy. Hold the apple in front of you, see its beautiful red color, and smell the aroma of God's fruit. Taste the splendor of the apple's inner juices. Chew each bite slowly and thoroughly, without rushing.

When one eats mindfully, one does so without consideration of time. Mindfulness takes us into the present moment where joy and happiness preside. When eating mindfully, don't chew your sorrow or suffering. Keep your mind clear and your attention focused on your present activity. Being mindful brings beauty and sacredness to whatever it is you are doing. In mindfulness, we are fully present, complete, and free of any worry or struggle. This is the way of calm and ease that an enlightened one seeks. You, too, can be mindful and enjoy the taste of freedom.

Mindfulness requires practice. You won't become a master overnight, but with daily practice, your abilities will improve. What stands in the way of becoming more mindful? Nothing more than the dominant mind patterns of human existence, which don't allow us to deep-dive into life. The endless mind noise of our thoughts distracts us from being truly present. If we can be silent and still on the inside, we can merge with the present moment and stay in presence for prolonged periods.

Take a Leap of Faith

I recently went snorkeling in the caves of Jamaica. My view from above showed clear water in most areas, but there were dark and mysterious parts as well. My experience required an initial jump off a twenty-foot seaside cliff and into the ocean. My fears were twofold. First, I needed to find the courage to jump off the cliff; second, my fear of the dark unknown regions of the water was greater than I initially thought. I soon realized my fears stood between me and my new experience. I needed to become fearless and fully present in the now before I made my jump. As I stood on the cliff, ready to dive into the ocean, I closed my eyes and began to meditate. I repeated this mantra aloud three times: "I dwell in the present moment. I feel the magnificence of this moment." When I opened my eyes, I was free of all fear, and I took a leap of faith off the cliff and into the ocean below. Once I came up to the surface, my wife, Olivia, gave me constant encouragement to put on my snorkeling mask and take a look beneath me. Reluctantly, I placed the mask over my face and looked down. My eyes must have been as big as quarters because the beauty I witnessed was incredible. The reef was teeming with beautiful exotic fish and stingrays. The dark spots I saw and feared from above were actually other beautiful reefs. Had I never found the courage to jump, I would have never seen the beauty underneath the mystery. By choosing to let go of my fears and taking a leap of faith, I was the beneficiary of a life-changing experience. Now I have put my fear of snorkeling behind me, and I can't wait for my next island adventure. I learned that fear often obstructs our life's progression. If we can overcome our fears, we can discover the hidden beauty that is contained inside each moment. This ocean experience forever changed me, and I am truly grateful.

You, too, can extract more out of your life by overcoming your fears and taking a leap of faith. What you have to gain is access to new dimensions inside you that create joy and freedom. Life is here to be lived, not suppressed. The best moments of life are those in which you must overcome an obstacle or fear in order to get where you want to be.

The Portal of the Now

For centuries, spiritual masters of all faiths have pointed to the now as the portal to the spiritual dimension. "The present moment (the Now) is the only portal into the timeless and formless realm of being," Eckhart Tolle wrote. By definition, a portal is a door, entrance, or threshold. This gateway to your soul is the secret entrance to your higher power and unlimited potential, the dimension of the greater you. The moment you grasp and master this concept, there will be a colossal shift from your mind to your inner being, from your location in time and place to the space of pure presence. When you are silent, focused, and acutely aware, you slip into presence. The present moment isn't something you find; it is the moment you cannot escape. An aware person's focus is always in the present moment, without references to the past or future. Speaking of past events takes you out of the present and back to your consciousness of the past. Speaking of the future also takes you out of the moment and into an existence that hasn't happened yet—and may never happen. Either way, the only thing that matters is what is happening right now. What lies ahead for you in the future is being created in the here and now. The goal is to become fully present in the now and in alignment with your inner essence. Be intimate with the present moment. By remaining in the present moment, all problems of your past and anxiety of the future are dissolved. All pain, suffering, and sorrow cannot exist in the miracle that is now. You are the living miracle, and the miracle starts with you simply being alive and able to breathe as a free person. Find gratitude for your next breath and keep your attention on the present moment for as long as you can.

When you focus on the now, the distractions of the past and the future diminish. The true power in life exists in the present moment. When you bring your attention and focus onto the now, it generates a force field around you that is the same energy that creates worlds. Anything unconscious dissolves in the light of presence. Choose to focus your attention inward toward the present moment, your elevator to the seat of your soul.

The Significance of Silence

Identifying with thoughts from your mind keeps you out of the now. To become fully present, you must quiet your mind. You may observe your thoughts as the witness of your experience, but don't judge what you observe. Sitting in silence and solitude allows the mind to rest, and the brain to let down its sensory guard. As Herman Melville once wrote, "All profound things and emotions of things are preceded and attended by silence." Silence is inherently therapeutic. A free being no longer identifies themselves by their thoughts, emotions, and memories. This limited version of you is known as the *mind-made self.* Enlightenment is the process of rising above your thoughts and finding freedom—liberation from the prison of a cluttered mind. To be enlightened is to see clearly and without distortion.

Turn Your Attention to Your Breath

Most people don't even realize they have become slaves to their minds. When higher consciousness settles in, there is a knowing that the mind knows little. While it can be almost impossible to shut off all your thoughts, it is possible to shift your focus away from your thoughts and feelings and onto your next breath. Let your attention follow each breath all the way into and all the way out of your body. Watch and feel your chest rise and fall, and feel the replenishment of energy to your body with each breath. Your breath is the bridge between your body and your soul. Don't try to control your breathing; simply allow it to be natural, and observe that it requires no effort at all. Many of your bodily functions, including your breath, are regulated independently of your mind by a mysterious inner power. Once your mind is quiet, shift your focus inward toward the stillness inside you that is your pure self.

Stillness

Many beautiful things arise out of stillness. Stillness is the chamber of the soul. "Be still. Stillness reveals the secrets of eternity," Lao-tzu wrote. Many spiritual masters have said that when you enter stillness, you awaken the divinity within you. What arises in stillness are your divine intelligence and unlimited potential. Your greatness lies in your ability to travel inward to your center, fully surrendering to what is presently happening. Ramana Maharshi once said, "All that is required to realize the Self is to be still. What can be easier than that?"

Finally, form and formless become one, held together by the supreme force of the universe. What is inevitable is a return home to your truth as the self. All that is unconscious about you will be brought into the light of consciousness. This awakened divinity in you is your true nature, the God essence in you. This spiritual process is known as *self-realization*. Know that you are pure loving awareness. This incredible shift of consciousness is transmuted into divine light. This newfound realized state of being is presence, the realm of timelessness and formlessness, and the space of your true identity beyond name and form.

Present-Moment Power

All forms of creation arise out of the present moment.
The more present you are in the moment, the more peaceful
you become. Meeting the heart of each moment opens
the soul to the majesty and power of life. Stay connected
with this spiritual place, and you will discover the beautiful
world of expansion. You are here to deliver your gift.
The deeper you go inside, the greater the gifts are.
Your gifts are your presence, purpose, song, and smile.

Our Mission

Our mission as human beings is to close the gap
between who we are showing up as every day
and who we really are as divine emanations of God.
This is the mission of the greater you.
This is the path to your soul.

Find Sacred Moments Each Day

What is spiritual to you is what you decide to dedicate
yourself to and to make sacred. Make conscious attempts
to turn special parts of your day into sacred moments for
the evolution of your soul. As the sun rises, acknowledge
your inner essence, and recite your intentions aloud and
also to others. Be present in the unification of your mind, body,
heart, and soul; this is presence. Your universal alignment
calls forth your inner power and the greatness within you.

New Life

I am welcoming into my body new life breathed into
my soul by the very joy of my heavenly experience here on
earth. I will allow the events of this day to unfold for me and
my greater purpose. Each moment that I am truly present is
an opportunity for my soul to grow and love deeper.

Surrender to the Present Moment

Don't block your experience by dwelling on what isn't
happening for you. Surrender to the present moment.
Your life is happening right now. Even though things may
appear the same as yesterday, they aren't unchanged.
Changes are occurring inside you every second of
every day, whether you perceive them or not. Don't focus
on what you're seeing; focus on how you would like to
feel, and your life experience will follow your vibration.

Where Love and Harmony Preside

Your enjoyment of the present moment is
every bit as important as living in the moment.
The thrill of life is present in the here and now.
Feel it, taste it, and experience it. Joy is the
background and the very fabric of this realm.
Underneath the waves of your life lies a symphony
of music where love and harmony preside. The
frequency and pitch of happiness surround you;
all you must do is tune in to its beautiful vibration.

Don't Miss the Present Moment

If you're constantly looking back into your past or focusing
too much on your future, you are missing the present
moment. The people and experiences
seeking you cannot reach you, because your mind isn't
focused on where you actually exist, which is in the present.
The present moment is where all things are created. If you
aren't living in the moment, then you may be missing your
breakthrough opportunity. Your life is unfolding right in front
of you. Be present and feel the immense power of now.

You Are Divine Love

Take off your shoes and feel the earth you walk on.
Seek silence, but hear the winds of change. Increase your
awareness of scents and fragrances to stimulate your mind.
Taste success, but don't fear failure. Listen to others as you
would like to be listened to. Always speak your truth.
Look through your inner eye and see yourself for who you really are.
You are divine love expressing itself as human consciousness.

Are You Willing to Look Inside?

Are you willing to look inside yourself?
All the answers to your problems lie within you.
Facing your hidden deficiencies can be difficult, but
the reward for doing so is exponentially great. Gaining true
insight and understanding of your own contribution to
your circumstances is both crucial and enlightening.
The success of your outcomes depends on your alignment
with Source. A deeper understanding of your truth
leads to bottomless gratitude and higher elevations.

CHAPTER 11

The Soul

The Timeless and Limitless Self

Your soul is an aspect of God that is uniquely you. Your soul is your formless nature. It is the essence of who you are. In the beginning, your soul chooses you. Sometimes your soul waits years or even lifetimes to incarnate with you in the manifested world. Your soul chooses you and your family so that it may achieve the experiences it needs in order to evolve. Your soul is always seeking to balance itself energetically. According to Hindu philosophy, your soul unites with your body in the womb between sixteen and twenty weeks of gestation. This time correlates with a mother's first perception of her unborn child's movement. Shortly after the soul unites with the body, a period of amnesia ensues.

Amnesia and Remembrance

The human mind is blocked from remembering aspects of the soul in order to focus on the development of the ego axis, which is critical in early childhood development. This intense body-mind focus blocks our perception of oneness with the soul and with God. This is why we are always in the state of remembering. Much of the suffering we experience here on earth is a direct result of falsely believing that we are separate from God and from one another. We are truly one with God, our fellow man, and the universe.

Healing from your condition is the process of remembering who you truly are. Your healing comes when your soul shines through and your personality sees your light and believes this light to be its true self. Your healing is complete with the recognition that you are the goodness of life and represent the greater good. Your soul is the purest form of self that can ever be. When you recognize your divine light, it expands internally, and, ultimately, shines externally so that others may see it and be inspired to shine. Your inner light shines brighter with each responsible choice you make, and so does the world you create. The brighter your inner light shines, the more it frees you from the bondage of fear and limitation. Your aura is always radiating the love and joy that reside deep inside your soul.

Prebirth Planning

Before your birth, there was much talk of bringing balance into your being. Your soul's evolutionary plan is often determined in prebirth planning sessions alongside spirit guides and other souls with whom you will share your incarnation. Guides are assigned to a particular soul before that soul's arrival on earth. Guides are our spiritual teachers who bring us love, comfort, and support. Everyone living on earth has a spirit guide.

Our guides work diligently to ensure we have the experiences we planned before birth, even when those experiences are painful.

In these prebirth planning sessions, the lessons we need to learn and the ways in which we intend to learn them are discussed. This is when soul agreements are made with other souls. We all belong to a group of souls who are parallel to us at the same evolutionary stage of development. A soul group is a cluster of souls who have evolved to a common energy vibration. These like-minded beings are frequently people in your inner circle, such as parents, siblings, teachers, and close friends. Often this group of souls has played different roles in your past incarnations to further your own evolution as well as the advancement of the entire group.

Certain challenges and experiences are planned to bring energetic balance into your being. Years ago, I believed the idea to write this book was conceived in this lifetime, but now I realize that I have simply remembered my prebirth planning. I now understand that my own spiritual awakening is actually a remembering of who I am as an infinite soul. At some level of our consciousness, we are able to remember the souls we plan to meet and create with in this lifetime. The experience of remembering hidden aspects of ourselves produces the fullest and most rewarding life journey possible.

When you meet members of your soul group, there is a feeling of familiarity, as if you have known them forever. This explains the sense of longing to be inseparable from certain members of your tribe. Members of a soul group have a common sense of purpose and bonding when they get together, and they are destined to evolve at a similar rate. Their presence in your life is always assisting you in your evolution. You are always awakening to the mission of your soul. When you use your gifts, life lessons, and essence to serve the world, you will awaken and inherit wisdom, joy, love, and peace everlasting.

Your Soul's Assignment

There is a higher purpose for your life, a calling. Buried deep within you is your soul's assignment, the thing you are called on to do in this lifetime. The moment you turn inward is when you will discover your true calling. Before you uncover your soul's mission, you must awaken to your divine self. There is a secret way of the soul; it is the way of love and peace. Your soul is your inner guidance system of divine intelligence, which works through you. It knows just what is needed and always supplies it at just the right time.

Living life at the level of your soul is the first step on the ladder to finding your higher purpose. Our souls are in constant communication with us, supplying us with yearnings, interests, and intuitions that lay the foundation for our future. A soul's balance is obtained by experiencing both light and darkness in each lifetime. Author Gary Zukav wrote, "The personality (ego mind) emerged as a natural force from the soul. It is an energy tool that the soul uses to function in the physical world."

One of the roles of your soul is to teach your ego what the soul already knows. In addition, the lessons your ego brings back to your soul are incorporated into your evolution. Your soul contains the personalities of all your past incarnations and thus has wisdom beyond your imagination. If you are unaware of your truth and deny that there is any level of higher wisdom and soul guidance available to you, then your guidance must come through the density of physical events. My mother, Dolly, referred to this as "learning the hard way." The easier path is the recognition and acknowledgment of the guidance from your divine soul. The more you act from this place of divinity, the more powerful and fulfilled you will be. Your soul is your inner energy field, which is always calling you home. Although your soul doesn't have a specific anatomical location, many experts claim the road to your soul is through your heart. *The Greater You* is a calling to live life from a heart-based consciousness.

"The being who fully realizes
their formless nature, is no
longer fooled by the ever-
changing forms of the
material world."

- Unknown

Shifting Your Identity from Your Ego to Your Soul

The identity shift from the ego to the soul happens through love. Because of the shift of identity to the soul, instead of seeing a burden, we see opportunity; instead of seeing our life challenges as punishment, we see purpose. In your new perspective, every disadvantage can be turned into an advantage. Your soul is derived from divine love, and it is your truth and inner light. Because your soul is pure love, your soul expands as you love deeper. Love changes energy fields and people. When people are in alignment with mind, body, heart, and soul, their energy can change the world. You and your soul are one. Your soul is always right there by your side, and you can always access its energy in one conscious breath.

Shower Mantra

Some people's focus is so fixed on the mind and body that the soul is often forgotten. It has been said that the reason a person feels unhappy or sad is because they have left their soul behind. In my morning routine, one of the first things I do is a shower mantra that starts my day. I inhale deeply through my nose and say aloud, "Good morning, Holy Spirit!" I repeat this phrase three times, along with three conscious breaths. This practice invigorates me and brings my physical body into alignment with my peaceful and loving nonphysical self. The entire process takes less than one minute, but the benefits of doing so last all day long. This alignment assures me that any decision or action I make that day is made from the perspective of my higher self. Feel free to adapt my shower mantra into your morning routine.

Alignment with Your Soul

You are a gifted soul living in a physical body. The precious gift of your body is that it gets to express itself fully in this leading-edge reality. It is here on earth that the evolution of souls takes place. Our human form is the part of us that contains fear and seeks power. This is because our human body isn't everlasting, and we fear our eventual death. The only way you can die in peace is to get in touch with that part of you that is already aligned with inner peace. The soul is the part of us that never dies. The soul is unborn and thus timeless and deathless. The soul doesn't contain fear because it is eternal. There is no uncertainty within the soul; there is only love and light. The sooner you unite with your higher self, the sooner fearlessness and abundance will find their way into your existence.

Now is the time to shift into alignment with your soul; there is no time like the present. Divine light is your nature, and it begins to call you toward it from the moment you are born. Your alignment with pure love repositions you, adjusts your altitude, and provides direction to your way. Your soul is your true nature; it is the part of you that you are required to remember and embrace. If you can align with your soul, you can access the part of you that contains infinite wisdom, love, joy, and everlasting peace.

You Are a Gifted Soul

You are a gifted soul living in a physical body. The precious gift of
the body is that your soul is allowed to express itself in the physical world.
The power of your being lies in your inner flow of pure consciousness.
In the very beginning, your soul chooses you. It aligns with you at birth and
learns from your life lessons. As the years go by, your soul evolves.
Your human form is the part of you that contains fear and seeks power.
This is because your human body isn't everlasting, and, thus, you live in
constant fear of your inevitable death. Your inner being is timeless and
deathless. Your nonphysical self doesn't contain any fear or worry,
because it is eternal. In death, your divine soul is liberated from your body;
it becomes untethered and is free to return home and into the arms of God.

It Is There for You

It is there for you. Open your loving heart, and what you shall find
there is the gate to your soul. Inside the hidden chambers of your
inner being lies your true greatness. Your soul is your glory; it is the
part of you that is infinite and everlasting. Your soul keeps your dreams
alive and gently guides you along your path. Your soul is your inner
identity and the aspect of God in you.

You and Your Soul Are One

Between our first days of life and our last dying breath,
we spend our lives searching for completeness.
The sequences of life are driven by your soul's attraction
to your beginning and your inevitable end.
You and your soul are one, a perfect vibrational match.
Your soul completes your being; you are it, and it is you:
soul power personified, oneness and love everlasting.

Your Soul Chooses You

Your soul wanted to be with you so badly that it was willing to wait for you.
A particular soul can wait years, sometimes several lifetimes, for
its perfect match. This divine agreement defines our existence.
Once your mind, body, and soul are united, your soul's agreement is fulfilled.
It is always a perfect match. Your mind and body give your soul the power
of expression here on earth. Whether a particular soul is with a body for
only a few days or over a whole lifetime, it is happy to physically
experience itself through you. Your soul is desperate to experience your
humanity and your unique presence. Your soul chooses you.

I Have Secrets to Tell You

I have secrets to tell, and so do you.
As souls, we are all born with gifts to share with the world.
We are all interconnected and driven by the purpose of our souls.
The illusion is happening whenever we hold the belief that
our journey is external and thus somehow outside ourselves.
The truth is that our greatest journey is internal, toward the call
of our souls. In divine order, each being will discover and unveil
their unique gifts, enabling them to place their piece of
the puzzle into the universal design of life.

This Is the Nature of a Soul's Evolution

You can believe the illusion for as long as it serves you,
but, sooner or later, you will discover that the purpose of your
earth reality is for your soul to grow and experience itself.
When your divine soul expands, so does the consciousness
of the universe. This is the nature of a soul's evolution.
As you continue your path toward enlightenment, you shed
your temporary false identity, known as the ego, and grow toward
the expression of your inherent truth. This path places you in
alignment with unconditional love and reunites you with
your highest wisdom and greater purpose.

Sounds of a Revolution

The sounds you hear stirring deep down in your soul are
sounds of a spiritual revolution. Your higher self is demanding
change and growth. Listen for the call of your inner voice;
it is the call of your soul. Like the transformation of a caterpillar
into a butterfly, struggle pushes your evolution toward liberation.
In transformation, you shed resistance and welcome
a world of freedom, peace, and love.

We Seek Approval

Sometimes we seek the approval of another person so much
that we imagine them as more desirable than they really are.
The less attention we get from them, the more we want from them.
Wanting and needing are two different things; fulfilling our desires
doesn't always fulfill a need. We must trust that the people we need to
assist us are already within our reach. We don't need to look
for them; they are already around us. The only attention that
we need to seek is a lasting love for ourselves.

The Presence of Your Loving Soul

Everything in this realm has a beginning and an inevitable end.
This earthly realm is a linear dimension in accordance with time.
Conversely, the soul is timeless and everlasting. The key to accessing
the power of your soul lies in residing in the present moment.
When you are tuned in and turned on to the power of now,
the vertical dimension in your life will appear. It is precisely
then that you may experience a vertical drop, like that of an elevator,
straight down into the bliss of pure awareness. In this dimension,
you can experience the presence and bliss of your loving soul.
The voice of your higher self is always a whisper, never a loud cry.
This voice of your soul is soothing and encouraging; it will lead you
toward sacred love and light. Recite this soul prayer whenever you
feel anger, uncertainty, fear, or confusion.

Soul Prayer

My soul is the center of my being. I am willing to accept the path of least resistance as light onto my very soul. Teach me, God, to follow the wisdom of my higher self. Stand by me and help me to recognize situations that are beyond my control. I understand that my positive attitude will always determine my altitude. I will start every morning with a single positive thought and build on it throughout each day. I embrace the notion that the law of attraction is the momentum behind my thoughts, which are seamlessly translated into form. May the love in my heart be my compass and my means of navigation throughout my spiritual journey. Let the smiles of each being I encounter reflect the light of God, and may each loving soul find their alignment in our magnificent universe. Grant me the power of vision to manifest my preferred outcomes, and let my faith bear witness to my dreams. Father God, may You know the depth of my gratitude for my very existence, and I pray that tomorrow's sunrise will deliver the presence and grace that my inner awakening requires.

Here are ten spiritual laws I live by; they have been useful in my life. Each law has helped me reach a state of wakefulness, and harmony with others and the entire universe. It is my hope that these spiritual laws will bring clarity and understanding to you on your journey.

Ten Spiritual Laws to Live By

1. Life is spiritual. Everyone has a soul made of pure love gifted from God.
2. We exist in a state of oneness. We are all connected. We are all equal. Every human soul is animated by the same Source energy.
3. Your physical body communicates by way of an electrochemical process. Because energy cannot be created or destroyed, it simply transforms. Your soul will exist forever in one energy state or another.
4. There is an aura and correspondent vibrational field that surrounds you at all times.
5. Your thoughts and emotions right now determine the condition of your spirit. Mindfulness matters.
6. When you connect with your soul, you tap into the ancient wisdom of your inner being and your infinite potential. Your universal alignment of mind, body, heart, and soul creates your most desirable vibration and flow.
7. Your purpose is to find and follow the path of least resistance, which leads you to your soul. Seek to connect spiritually with others. You are here to deliver your unique gift to the world. This is also known as your greater purpose.
8. Transformation is the doorway and process that advances your transition to a soul-based identity.
9. The power of love, creation, choice, and surrender are your greatest powers.
10. Love is the language of your soul.

CHAPTER 12

Love

Love Is the Answer

The Bible says, "God is love." Clearly, God created love, in that He alone defines what love is. Love is knowing you are more than flesh, because the Creator has provided you a soul and assigned it to your body. You are a spark of the Divine, filled with sacred love and light. As a divine emanation of God consciousness, you are filled with love. His love and light are always with you in life and also in death. You are inseparable from Him. As we each enter the physical world, we become love temporarily hidden from itself.

The first part of our spiritual journey is remembering who we really are. As beings of light, our true essence is unseen by the body mind and thus unrealized. When we do remember who we are as the self, soul consciousness expands, and our inner light shines forth for all to see. This is why we are here: to remember our true nature. Each being is divine love personified. Everyone is blessed with the gift of life and leaves their imprints on humanity and consciousness itself.

When you act from the space of unconditional love, without consideration of receiving love in return, blessings begin to flow. When love is filtered through your mind, it becomes conditioned and weakened. The sun shines not only for itself but also to warm the earth. The sun transfers its brilliant energy outward, without the possibility of receiving any light in return. This is what love is; love is unconditional and free. Similar to the sun, you are also a light of love. When you share your love, you share your loving light. Unconditional love isn't consumption; it is a sacrifice and surrender to a cause other than yourself. You control your own light. You control the flow of your love. Live boldly and love unselfishly. What this world needs more of, is your unconditional love.

Self-Love

Self-love and a healthy self-image are keys to self-preservation. Your mental picture of yourself has a powerful effect on your future. Failure to love yourself enough results in stress, fear, anger, and frustration. We must all learn to love whatever arises in us. Don't ever hate yourself or your life; if you do, you will discover that it is only a tool of self-destruction. Hate turns good people into victims. Be compassionate toward yourself, love each and every part of yourself, and remember to treat yourself tenderly. You are one magnificent miracle! You are an expression of love born from consciousness itself. We awaken to our hearts by loving the aspect of ourselves that has been hurt by neglect, abuse, or emotional pain. The cleansing action of loving oneself fully transmutes the cellular memory of past pain and suffering. Healing opens the heart space and ushers in the ability to love once again.

To anyone who has ever loved and lost, take a minute to say this mantra aloud; it is designed to send healing energy to your broken heart.

Love Mantra (read aloud)

I am not merely my past experiences.
I am not my broken heart.
I am open to healing my past wounds.
In my healing, I welcome abundant love
into my heart and soul.
I am both resilient and strong.
I deserve to be loved.
I will share my love with the world.

The Ego Resists Unconditional Love

Although love is your natural state, this keen awareness has been deeply buried by the ego. The ego is not a fan of unconditional love because the ego seeks power. Thus, ego death results in the self-realization that you are indeed love itself. Because of the conflicting dynamic between the ego and the soul, the ego resists your alignment with the self at every turn. This is the reason why so many loving relationships are sabotaged by the ego.

The ego is never satisfied and always wants more of everything. I call this syndrome the *disease of more.* The ego desires more money, clothes, shoes, cars, attention, and admiration, when all we really need is more love. The more we are aligned with our truth, the greater our ability to love deeper becomes. A major concern in your life should be your alignment with love. The space between you and that alignment is the distance from you to your heart. The farther you move away from your heart, the more deeply your mind can influence you. If you get trapped by the spell of your mind, you may never get free to create life out of pure love. The way you get into alignment with love is to put down the notion that love is somehow outside of who you are. Love is your true nature; it is the aspect of you that grows with every action of gratitude, compassion, and understanding that you exercise.

Love Is a State of Being

Love is often misinterpreted as an emotion. In reality, love is not an emotion, because it is the vessel that contains all other emotions. In the grasp of love, all emotion is turned into light. Enter the space where you can download the program called Love; the cost is free. Love is a beautiful space of nonjudgment surrounded by the fragrances of vulnerability and trust. Love is a state of being of the highest order. Life is love masquerading as life.

Love is the melting of the heart, which lights your soul on fire. A soul on fire is a soul fully awake and realized. Truth will burn away all remaining aspects of personhood that continue to obscure the self. When the fire of a soul burns at its brightest, it can be seen from afar. This is when you can attract your soul mate. A true love can start a fire that burns so brightly it makes everything else seem unimportant.

Freedom and love go together.
Love is not a reaction. If I love you because you love me,
that is mere trade, a thing to be bought in the market;
it is not love. To love is not to ask anything in return,
not even to feel that you are giving something-
and it is only such love that can know freedom.

—Jiddu Krishnamurti

Soul Mates

Meeting my wife and soul mate, Olivia, changed my entire life. Before I met Olivia, my relationships existed at a superficial level. Whenever I pushed toward a deeper level of love, something scared me, and I retreated. Because of my retreats, these relationships dried up like the fruit of a neglected tree. Retrospectively, what held me back each time was the whisper of my soul, which had a better plan for me.

Recognizing the potential of an everlasting love with Olivia, I took a leap of faith and dove deep into the abyss of unconditional love. I ceased to worry about how things would work out and surrendered to love. Because of this leap of faith, I found a deep space of vulnerability in my heart that I had never felt before. The more I opened myself to experience life without fear, the deeper in love I fell. My admiration for her turned into respect, and my affection for her turned into surrender.

We found a common purpose and began to manifest life's treasures at will. She brought inspiration into my life, and our unity became the fertile ground for many successes and dreams come true. Amid the evolution of our love, we took sacred vows, thus beginning the spiritual journey of unconditional love. My love for her traveled so deeply into my heart that my heart felt like it would explode. I can recall my spirit lighting up when just thinking about her beautiful traits, and I thank God for her presence in my life.

True love is a beautiful and wonderful thing that goes on forever. Relationships that don't pass the test of time aren't true love; they are more likely infatuations or even illusions in one's mind. Love is not desire or pleasure. True love endures. Far beyond the end of time, when there is nothing left, love will still remain. Love is beautiful and amazing, yet perfectly flawed. Love is acceptance and requires the practice of devotion to reach its highest potential. Love requires patience; you can admire from afar, but to truly love someone, you must be fully open and present.

Love is a commitment to the bond between two souls that is unbreakable. Everyone gets lonely. Every heart needs another heart. Everyone needs another somebody. Real work is done in pairs. One must be willing to sacrifice individual wants and needs for the greater good of the relationship. To maintain a loving dynamic, each partner must have respect for the other. Without respect for your lover, there can be no love. Love is a verb, an action word, but one's actions better measure it. The perfume rising out of a hug is love, but love isn't the action of the hug itself. Perhaps a hug is an act of closeness, compassion, empathy, or even affection; but true love is a state of being.

You become your own soul mate by loving yourself from the inside out. Until then, you are going to manifest more relationships that end in failure. Love is the heart's expression of your truth revealed; it radiates from the center of all beings. Everyone is capable of sharing a great love, but, first, you must love yourself.

The Cheat Code for Life

The cheat code for life is L.O.V.E.
L is for the start of a love revolution inside your heart.
O is for the obliteration of negative thought patterns.
V is for the vision of who you wish to become.
E is for the evolution of your soul.

Supreme Love

Some people love out of desperation, loneliness, or attachment; this is something else disguised as love. Real love is unconditional and experienced at the depth of one's soul. The highest form of love is pure bliss, which results from the expression of absolute joy. Only those who are willing to surrender their ego can experience this supreme love. Someone once said, "Love is freely giving someone access to rip your heart out but having faith that they won't." There are so many different interpretations of love, and everyone sees and feels it differently, but one thing is true for everyone—love is real.

TRIANGLE
OF LOVE

BLISS

LIGHT	JOY	PRESENCE
UNITY	FIRE	TIMELESS
ACCEPTANCE		VIRTUOUS
PURPOSE	TRUST	SWEETNESS
FORGIVENESS	CREATION	PURITY
SACREDNESS	HEALING	BOND
UNPREDICTABLE	UNCONDITIONAL	BEAUTIFUL
VULNERABILITY		FRAGRANCE
UNDERSTANDING	HONESTY	TOGETHERNESS
SACRIFICE	COMMITMENT	PATIENCE
FEARLESSNESS	RESPECT	SPONTANEOUS
SUPPORT		COMPROMISE
AMAZING	KINDNESS	FUN
ENJOYMENT		PASSION
AFFECTION	LEAP OF FAITH	ADMIRATION

COMPANIONSHIP

Love Is Bending the Universe Toward Light

Love is bending the universe toward light.
With every act of kindness, compassion, and love, we are
creating a force that is stronger than any known resistance.
This pushes earth's society toward unity and global peace.
As we acknowledge the presence of hate and indifference,
let our hearts remain pure, and let our intentions be known.
This universe belongs to those who live and let love.

Nothing Evolves Us Like Love

Embrace the unconditional love that resides in your heart.
It is there that you will find your inner peace. Serenity is the
whisper of love's beautiful voice. Love's call is a gentle
caress of your soul to awaken. Love is the most powerful
force in the universe, and its appearance in your life is
a calling to come alive. What the world needs now is for
more souls to come alive. When we awaken to love,
we awaken to our truth. Nothing evolves us like love.

Love Is the Easy Way Forward

Who said that spiritual growth is hard to do?
It's easy; we make it difficult. Love is the way;
the way is love. Love is the easy way forward.
Love is the heart's expression of your very truth revealed.
Love reshapes energy, and love transforms souls.
Love is more than capable of bending reality.
When you serve love from your infinite heart space, your
path to a more joyful life is only a heartbeat away.

Love Always Endures

There are only a few forces that can alter your life.
Love is one such force. Love can change your life and elevate
your consciousness, as well as the hearts and souls
surrounding you. The divine power of love is simply unlimited.
Love transforms hearts and rebuilds souls. Love always endures.
Far beyond the end of time, when there's nothing left, love will still remain.

Give Yourself Permission to Love

When you drop your fears, attachments,
and illusions, you will know what love is.
Give yourself permission to fall in love far beyond
measure. What you find there is what you are seeking.

Real Work Gets Done in Pairs

In our search for true love, we sometimes block the arrival
of that love. We hold a stout position in our minds of
what we think love should be and when it should arrive.
We have specific expectations, and then we posture ourselves
in a rigid way. The alternative is to become better receivers of
love's frequency and allow our lives to become reflections of
not what we desire but what we need. The journey of our hearts
should be much less rational and far more spontaneous.
Just remember that real work gets done in pairs.

Self-Love

We have always had a promise in place,
a promise to uphold a love for ourselves.
This is the level of self-love we are committed to.
Failure to love oneself enough results in sadness,
dysfunction, and personal suffering. There's so much
power in love. Love is universal; it is always there for us.
Embrace it, believe it, and be it.

Our Capacity to Love

If your heart ever gets overwhelmed with sadness and pain,
you can die of a broken heart. Sometimes, deep down in
our ego self, we come to feel undeserving of great love.
We begin to doubt the quality of the love we do receive,
and question its authenticity and sustainability. Regretfully,
we often turn down promising new opportunities of love to
avoid ever being hurt again. Forgiveness can cure heartbreak.
The time for change is here and now. We can still have the
life we once envisioned. It's time to let go of dark thinking
to risk our hearts once again for a chance at love. Love is
all we need. Our capacity to love is directly related to our
ability to forgive, forget, be vulnerable, and be loved.

Start Your Day with an Act of Love

(Read aloud)
Start your day with an act of love.
There is no better way to begin each morning.
Breathe in deeply the freshness of morning dew.
Hear the birds high in the trees singing their stories.
See the hummingbird hover effortlessly above.
Smell the fragrance of nearby orchids.
Touch the rich black soil to absorb its power.
Live each moment alive and free.
Share the gift of love with your smile.
Keep the faith that all is well.
Dream a dream you can remember.
Finish your day with an act of compassion.

CHAPTER 13

Gratitude and Compassion

The Healing Journey

Life is beautiful, and so are you. The majestic qualities of life are divinely inherent. Our very breath is what nourishes our bodies and supplies oxygen to our minds. The blessed nature of life touches us all, but, sooner or later, storms will confront us. We all must endure our challenges, and we must do so with courage and faith. To survive the rough patches in life, we must courageously pass through them. When we come out on the other side of our crisis, we must embrace the transformed person we have become in the process. How you evolve as a result of your crisis is equally as important as surviving your pain. Many people never overcome their struggle with life. Some people carry the burden of their pain with them every day and see their lives through the narrow lens of the victim. Victimhood robs you of gratitude and humility. It is far healthier to see yourself as a survivor instead of a victim. It is favorable to see everything in your life as a teachable moment. Now is the time to take back your power and position as a pilot of change. The goal is to turn your misfortune into motivation, to trade in your naïveté for wisdom, and to turn your uncertainty into purpose.

In today's world, there are more people suffering from stress, anxiety, depression, and psychosis than ever before. Our complex society is evolving at a rapid rate. As humans, we must learn to cope more effectively with the cumulative effects of daily stress on our health. When we struggle, our physicians are quick to prescribe a wonder pill to cure our ills. Major drug companies are registering record profits from the sale of antidepressants, antianxiety agents, and antipsychotic medications. Pharmaceutical companies literally make billions of dollars off the suffering of their customers. While these medications help many people get out of bed each morning, very few advancements have come in the form of alternative healing methods. Meanwhile social workers, psychologists, and psychiatrists have become overrun and cannot meet the increasing demands for psychological care.

The world is literally in need of emotional healing. As a result, we must learn how to cope and heal ourselves from our emotional ills and painful pasts. In my thirty-year career in medicine, I have had a close-up view of numerous patients who have successfully overcome their physical and emotional struggles. These survivors achieved a level of inner peace in their lives that very few others have experienced. As a result of interviewing, listening to, and treating thousands of patients in pain, I have developed what I call The Healing Journey. This is comprised of eight distinct stages of psychosocial advancement toward physical and emotional healing.

Step One: Forgiveness

We need to forgive those responsible for our painful past, and, most importantly, we must forgive ourselves. Many victims get stuck at this first step and never improve. If we are unable to forgive the people we hold responsible for our pain, we get stuck with the weight of carrying the load ourselves for the rest of our lives. The act of forgiveness lightens our load, frees us, and places us in the position of power. Forgiveness dissolves the pain of the past and brings our energy into the present moment. All healing takes place in the now; no healing has ever taken place in the past. Holding a grudge doesn't make a person stronger; it makes them bitter. Forgiving doesn't make a person weak; it sets their soul free. Forgiveness is a form of self-love. Nelson Mandela once said, "When a deep injury is done, we never heal until we forgive."

Step Two: Acceptance

When we are fully able to accept our circumstances, we inherit the power needed to change them. Every person's greatest power lies deep inside themselves. Most people tend to blame their circumstances on someone else. Blame is quite convenient and enables us to assume the role of the victim. A victim mentality is like a prison without walls, from which there is no escape. My grandmother used to say that the hardest prisons to break out of are the ones that we build around ourselves. We must summon the necessary strength and courage to assume full responsibility for our lives. Then and only then can we change our conditions and march toward freedom.

Once people can accept total responsibility for their journey, the ground beneath them solidifies and becomes firm and stable. It is from this position that a person can climb up the ladder of healing toward wellness. Acceptance of one's circumstances isn't disabling; it is actually empowering and strengthens one's ability to assume control over one's life. Repeat this affirmation: "I hereby accept my circumstances of today and take full responsibility for my current situation. I will no longer blame myself or anyone else for my condition, and I declare myself free from this affliction."

Step Three: Gratitude

Thankfulness for the gift of life itself and gratefulness for all blessings allow one to shift emotions away from one's condition and toward appreciation. Our gifts are many, but when a person is burdened by their struggle, there is a tendency for that person to focus only on their problems and not on their blessings. The greatest gift of all is life itself. At birth, we are ordained with the powers of creativity and choice, which means we always have the ability to change the way we feel. The power of gratitude lifts our spirits, shifts our focus, and attracts abundance to our lives. Speaking our blessings aloud creates an immediate mood shift by creating a higher vibration in our center. This change of frequency lifts us up out of darkness and places us in alignment with love and light.

We must not only be great in life, but also be grateful. The health benefits of practicing gratitude are endless. The health benefits of practicing gratitude are endless. Gratitude helps people to feel more positive emotions and decreases toxic emotions like sadness, envy, regret, and anger. Medical studies show that people who practice gratitude on a regular basis are happier, more optimistic, more relaxed, more spiritual, and more resilient in life. Consequently, grateful individuals have deeper relationships, show overall improvements in their health, and demonstrate more energy and greater longevity. In summary, gratitude facilitates a greater sense of well-being and a more positive mood. Therefore, if your vibration is off today, start counting your blessings and verbally say aloud what you are thankful for. Look for a lift and a shift, and welcome new energy into your life.

Step Four: Compassion

When we identify with the pain and struggle in other human beings and act on our instincts to help, we create a momentum of positive energy. The universe replies by multiplying this goodwill and shining light onto the darkest circumstances. Compassion, empathy, and understanding allow us to see ourselves in others, activating the power of oneness. In oneness, we become unified as one inseparable entity. The power of oneness is far greater than the power of one person. Oneness is capable of changing mind-sets, societies, countries, and the consciousness of the world.

The Way of Humility (read aloud)

In my struggle, I realize I'm not the only one affected by my condition. Many others have suffered my experience, and even more have endured far worse. I see myself in the eyes of those who have passed this road before me, and I open myself up to understand their struggle and what it took for them to endure their pain. I stand tall in the light of compassion, and I offer them my empathy and my heart.

Step Five: Faith

When you have faith in your life, you are never alone. Have the courage to step out in faith. When you place your trust in a power greater than you, it provides security, support, and buoyancy for your journey. Faith is the key that opens all doors. With faith, the impossible instantly becomes possible. When a person walks by faith, they walk with certainty and confidence. Having conviction is like riding the crest of a giant wave all the way to the shore. Faith elevates and empowers people to do certain things they ordinarily are unable to do. The Bible says faith is "more precious than gold that perishes" (1 Peter 1:7). It has long been said that faith ushers in salvation. When we step out in faith, the action of surrender brings about serenity and inner peace. Peace is the place that exists in the harmony of oneness with God. When we maintain faith in life, we create the space for miracles to occur on our behalf. All we must do is believe and let God do the rest.

Step Six: Reenergizing

You are a powerful being of unlimited and everlasting light. Sometimes the pain in our lives causes us to focus only on our painful bodies. In truth, you are not the body. The body is like a musical boom box. The box itself doesn't create the music it plays; it only projects the music out of its speakers. Once you have activated the powers of forgiveness, acceptance, gratitude, and compassion, you will be able to climb farther up the ladder of wellness. Climbing requires energy. You must stoke the fire for your journey with the most powerful source of healing: the power of love. Love is energy. Fill yourself up to capacity with love. Love yourself more, love your partner deeper, hug your children more often, and show greater love for your fellow man.

Create magical moments by following your joy. When you pursue your passion, joy can begin to fill the cracks of your pain. When you don't follow your joy, your mind tends to focus on what you don't have instead of on what you do have. This results in stress and feelings of scarcity. Shortage consciousness gives people the only excuse they ever needed to fail. Keep your thoughts positive, and more positive outcomes will come your way. Revitalize your mind and spirit through art appreciation, beautiful music, singing, dancing, walks in nature, and making love.

Step Seven: Wellness

To be in good health, one must be in alignment with the mind, body, heart, and soul. A healthy mind is one that remains positive regardless of outside conditions. Positive thinking must quickly replace negative thinking. Positivity acts to brighten our outlook for the future. The human body thrives on motion. Exercise is an important component of overall wellness. We are all familiar with the expression "Use it or lose it." If we allow the body to stagnate through prolonged periods of inactivity, unused parts will atrophy quickly and die. Stay active, and place yourself in nature as often as possible by walking on the beach, hiking, and swimming.

If your physical body can't perform any exercise, stay busy practicing mindfulness. Being mindful is being fully aware of what is happening right now, without wishing it were different. In mindfulness, the goal is to relax the body while performing daily routine activities. Equally important for total body wellness is rest and sleep. Try to create a balance in your life between activity, exercise, rest, and sleep. The human body requires periods of deactivation in order to heal and reenergize. Failure to get the proper rest results in energy depletion, illness, and mental breakdowns.

Make sure you drink water often to avoid dehydration and exhaustion. A well-balanced diet is also crucial to recovery and optimal health. Avoid sugary drinks and any unhealthy food choices that are frozen or come in boxes and bags. Choose natural fruits and vegetables over processed foods, and keep your caloric intake below two thousand calories per day. Your body is a temple that is irreplaceable. Don't abuse it; worship it.

Living at the level of your soul involves choosing love at every turn. When we act with love in mind, we are in alignment with Source; this is the essence of heart-based consciousness. At the end of our journey here on earth, the soul leaves the body and ascends to another dimension. When we learn to live from the platform of the infinite soul, we assume the identity of timeless beings. This strengthens our faith and resolve. When we are successful at shifting our identity from the ego to the soul, we begin to reflect our true nature as ageless, infinite, loving, and peaceful beings.

Step Eight: Grace

Living at the level of your soul leads you into the state of presence. Presence is having peace of mind and love in your heart, and fully surrendering to what is. This is also known as grace. A graceful being is one who moves through life with a loving and peaceful presence. Grace isn't a state of being to work toward but a gift from above for having mastered the essence of life. Grace is also the divine energy that assists your spiritual journey.

There is a force of supreme intelligence, beyond words, that always supports you and floats you in your beingness. When this earthly journey ends for you, you leave this realm with the same consciousness you acquired during this lifetime. This earthly plane is the place to awaken to your divinity, and now is the time for your awakening.

The Gift of Presence (read aloud)

I am here to awaken to the greater consciousness that is within me. I come with imperfections and impurities, and I am here to transcend them and embrace the God force within me. I choose to release my identification with all things that come and go so that I may be free to align with presence, which is my divine gift from heaven above.

Healing from your painful past is possible only by working through your psychosocial issues of today. We are all healers by nature, but the most difficult healing you will ever encounter is the resuscitation of your spirit. A key to healing is to visualize your healing as already done. Claim your peace, and support your vision of wellness by not speaking or acting in opposition to it. As people grow older, it is common to hear them list their medical conditions and proudly recite their numerous medications. The more you identify with your mind, the farther away you are pushed from your transition into eternal love and light. The healing journey is complete when your present condition doesn't limit your definition of yourself. See yourself as the everlasting and infinite soul. Instead of seeing yourself as a victim of life, see yourself as pure consciousness in human form experiencing life itself.

THE HEALING LADDER

WELLNESS

GRACE

RE-ENERGIZE

FAITH

COMPASSION

GRATITUDE

ACCEPTANCE

FORGIVENESS

Rockets of Intention

When you suffer emotionally, you fall victim to the idea that you are powerless in a particular situation. The truth is that the scenario you are currently experiencing is either from your direction or the result of your lack of direction. If you fail to visualize and create your own future, it will result in a change to a less favorable path. Your psychological well-being depends on the quality of your thoughts. When you are in crisis, seek alignment by practicing mindfulness and maintaining thoughts of bottomless gratitude. When you focus on gratitude, you are launching rockets of intention in the direction of mercy and grace.

Hidden Moments

There are hidden moments in everyone's daily life that are simply extraordinary. These occasions contain pure vibratory bliss. Recognize these events when they occur and hold on to them tightly in your memory. Take the opportunity to pour yourself deeper into these simple joyful experiences and be more appreciative of your amazing journey. The beautiful moments in your day are opportunities to increase the joy inside your ever-expanding heart, and also to deepen your appreciation for the extraordinary gift of life.

Don't Block Your Blessings

If you see the world as a threatening place,
then you will be unable to enjoy all of its beautiful offerings.
If you live each day in fear of what might happen to you,
then you will block your blessings. A bounty of unthinkable splendor is available to all those who can see the hidden delights in their daily lives. Take time to appreciate how fortunate you are for your very existence and be grateful for your divine blessings. Gratitude and love are true essentials in this world, and they are both gateways to the treasure of our universe.

Patience Is Love

When you are angered by someone's ignorance,
try to replace your anger with compassion.
Compassion is an expression of higher love.
No being is superior to another, we are all equal.
Conflicts are opportunities in your life to expand
your consciousness. The anger you feel inside
is because you see in it the same weaknesses
that you see in yourself.

The Circle of Compassion

To have a truly great journey, one must also serve others.
Don't just reach for individual success; inspire others to succeed
as well. Widen your circle of compassion. Your destiny is bound to
the destiny of us all; we are all interconnected. When you feel
compelled to serve humanity, shine your light in the direction of
universal compassion. Be generous with your love, without the
expectation of recognition or gratitude in return. What you learn,
share; and what you know, teach. Love yourself but also love
everything and everybody. Whenever you give unselfishly to others,
you create a greater space for your own personal growth and expansion.

When You Encounter a Wounded Soul

When you encounter a wounded soul, treat them with love and compassion.
Your attention may be the very medicine that heals them and makes them
feel whole again. Whenever compassion comes calling, answer the phone.
When someone needs a lift, give them a smile. Open your heart to touch
those who are untouchable. Bring food to the table to those who are hungry.
Provide shelter to those who can't protect themselves. Hope for the success
of others as you do for yourself. Give love to those incapable of loving
themselves. Share your gifts with those who need them most.

When One Soul Rises, We All Rise

When you're done practicing your own spirituality today,
say a prayer filled with love, understanding, and
healing for those who cannot support themselves.
Compassion opens the door to the soul. When something
valuable falls out of your pocket, whether it be damaged,
stained, or broken, pick it up; you will benefit from doing so.
As compassionate beings, we must also pick each other up
when we fall from grace. When you open your heart to
souls that fail in our society or fail themselves, you can
make a difference in their lives. Every soul is valuable on
this earth; every person matters. The gift is in the assist.
When one soul rises, we all rise.

There Is Freedom in Forgiveness

We are quicker to forgive others than we are to forgive ourselves.
When others hurt us, we frequently harbor unresolved
emotional pain. This is true even if we are innocent victims.
This feeling of guilt creates a roadblock to our emotional healing.
To heal from our painful past, we must forgive those responsible,
and we must also forgive ourselves. This liberates us from our pain
and creates space for deep healing to occur. Don't let your unpleasant
memories hold you back from your brilliant future. Forgive yourself,
forgive everyone else, and start experiencing the joy freedom brings.

There Is No Such Thing as Impossible

(Read aloud)
I am drawing inspiration today from
the power of Mother Earth herself.
I can feel the boundless natural electricity of
this amazing planet resonating underneath me.
When the energy waves upsurge into my body
through the soles of my feet, I feel rejuvenated.
As the earth's vitality flows through my veins
toward my heart, I reconnect with Source energy.
I am grateful for this day, moment, love,
and life. There is no such thing as impossible
and no greater opportunity than right now.

CHAPTER 14

Well-Being

The Body Is the Temple of the Soul

Those who wish for wellness, should embody the idea of total health. The right mental and spiritual practices nurture a happy, healthy consciousness. The ultimate state of well-being is the healthy unification of mind, body, heart, and soul. *Merriam-Webster* defines *well-being* as "the state of being happy, healthy, or prosperous." The science of well-being always begins with harmony and alignment with our inner being. There are many people who look incredible from the outside, but they are lost internally. A healthy body and a broken spirit serves no one. Health and happiness radiate from the inside out, not the outside in.

Elevating Your Mood

Coexisting states of calm, love, gratitude, and joyfulness characterize a happy state of being. Joy is the preferred state. Although remaining joyful isn't always possible, it is the presence of contrasting states, such as fear and sadness, that makes the feeling of joy so amazing. We must take the necessary steps to elevate our mood but also find ways to reduce the incidence of low-frequency thoughts, emotions, and behaviors. When we elevate our consciousness, we cast light on our path, which translates to feeling a joyful presence in our being. Our spiritual practice is the most important factor in our overall goal of wellness. The practice of mindfulness deepens our presence in the now and ushers in a higher state of awareness.

Energy Levels

Practicing thoughts of gratitude increases the fullness of life. Be grateful for the gift of being alive. Staying in the present moment doesn't allow you to remain unconsciously trapped in your past or future. When you reside in the now, your consciousness is liberated from thought, and you get into alignment with your higher self. Your energy state is directly correlated to the level of function of the cells in your body. In a joyful state, there is a rise of cellular energy and an enhancement of your inner energy field. You will also obtain optimal results when you are consistent with your spiritual practice, whether it be yoga, meditation, mindfulness, or prayer. Remember that your energy levels coincide with your distance from Source energy. The more time you spend in alignment with Source, the better you will feel.

The Body Temple

The body is the temple of the soul, so to achieve total wellness, you must respect and not neglect the body. If a body is well maintained, the aging process is slowed. To reach optimal health, one must also exercise the body. The benefits of exercise are well known. They include mood elevation, weight loss, reduction in cardiovascular disease, reduction of diabetes, strengthening of bones and muscles, and decreased rates of colon, endometrial, breast, and lung cancers. These all increase overall well-being and result in a prolongation of life. Being as active as you can possibly be improves your overall health and reduces your risk of obesity. While exercising the body is important, maintaining a healthy diet is also critical.

Organic Foods and Water

In the past, organic foods were only found in health food stores; now they are a regular feature at all supermarkets. The word *organic* refers to how farmers grow and process fruits, vegetables, grains, dairy, and meat. Organic farming practices also encourage soil and water conservation and reduce pollution. Compared to its counterparts, organic produce contains fewer pesticides and toxins that are harmful to the human body. Organically raised animals aren't given antibiotics, growth hormones, GMOs (genetically modified organisms), or animal by-products. Although eating organic is much healthier for you, it is also considerably more expensive. Price aside, making a commitment to healthy eating is a great start toward a healthier life.

One cannot speak about health without mentioning the benefits of drinking water. According to the *Journal of Biological Chemistry,* the human body is made up of approximately 60 percent water. When you drink water, you are drinking the essence of your existence. In the United States, water is the second most popular beverage, behind soft drinks. Many people believe that drinking any liquid is equal to reaping the benefits of water, but this assumption is untrue. Soft drinks and other sugary drinks represent a huge health hazard and are linked to increased incidences of obesity, diabetes, and strokes. Drinking water instead of soda can significantly reduce these risks.

The benefits of drinking more water are commonly known, but

let's take a moment to review them. Hydration has a major positive effect on energy levels and brain function. More specifically, water improves mood and decreases fatigue. Water also flushes out toxins, improves digestion, and helps prevent constipation. Water assists in weight loss and treats headaches and migraines. It is advisable to drink a glass of water when you first wake up and then drink multiple glasses throughout the day. It is also important to drink water during your meals, as this assists in digestion. Many people have said, "You are what you eat," but don't forget that you are also what you drink.

The Practice of Peacefulness

While the benefits of exercise and nutrition increase your well-being, paying attention to your emotions is also important. Start each day with positive affirmations and intentions to set your attitude. Try to find tranquillity during each day. Keep your conversations calm and peaceful. There is healing in serenity. The daily practice of silence creates a peaceful mind.

Peace of mind is priceless. Practice peace by being peaceful to others and yourself. Visualize peaceful projects and peaceful outcomes. Let go of troublesome memories, because the past no longer exists. Inner peace is always available to you. There is nothing wrong with pampering yourself to generate feelings of calm and ease. Treat yourself regularly to soothing massages, silent meditations, calming music, and the sweet songs of poetry. All these practices will generate beneficial effects for your overall health and wellness. Place yourself in nature as often as possible. When you see the boundless beauty of nature, the higher self is awakened. Engaging all five of your senses truly allows you to fully experience the awesome energy of the planet. You will find peace by staring at the ocean, taking a walk on the beach, or watching a beautiful sunset. Peace follows those who place themselves in peaceful situations.

Stay in Alignment with Love

Low-frequency emotions of sadness, disappointment, and regret can lead to anxiety and depression. Check your emotional current several times a day and eliminate any factors that consistently lower your vibration. You are in charge of the way you feel. Sometimes it's necessary to clear negative energy in your life, which may involve distancing yourself from a dear friend or loved one who is mired in negativity. Beware of the energy vampires in your life who consume much of your time and energy, but offer little in return. No one has the right to trample through your garden with disregard for your feelings or time. It is always your right and duty to protect your vibration. You must also learn to recognize enablers. Enablers are the feeders of another human's destruction. They are the ones who feel a certain gain from their participation in the acceleration of another person's demise.

Surround yourself with loving souls who provide you with the inspiration, strength, and encouragement you need to perform at your highest level. Seek out friends and relationships rooted in love, not competition. There is no living entity that the presence of more love doesn't enhance. Live love now and spread your loving light across the world.

The Joy of Your Soul

Close your eyes and center yourself.
Take three cleansing breaths and
visualize a beautiful, relaxing location;
imagine yourself there right now.
See yourself enjoying your calm surroundings.
Allow your facial muscles to relax, and smile.
All is well, and everything is as it should be.
Enjoy the increase of your vibration, and
appreciate the wave of wellness coming your way.
Draw nearer to your center in peaceful silence.
You have just experienced the joy of your soul.

Everything Is All Right

Everything is all right.
You are right where you are supposed to be.
All good things happen in time. You don't have to
search for your path; your path is always at your feet.
When you fall into acceptance of where you are,
you find presence and grace along the way.

Nothing Compares to You

Your competitive spirit is an inherent trait.
This is your survivor instinct rising. When you compare
yourself to your peers, you can get lost and lose your own
direction. In spite of your flaws, you're beautiful just
the way you are. The very trait you envy in someone
may, in fact, be that person's tragic flaw. Your individuality
is what makes you unique. It is pointless to compare
yourself to anyone else. You may not be perfect, but
you are truly one of a kind and irreplaccable.
Don't try to catch up; just show up.

The Soul Is an Ego-Free Zone

There is a hunger that burns deep inside you
for a conscious connection with your soul.
Unlike your hunger for food or thirst for water,
your greatest need is to be loved. The ego knows
that its reign will be over in this lifetime. Unlike your
personality, the soul is evolved beyond measure.
The soul is an ego-free zone; it possesses infinite wisdom.
Take steps in the direction of your loving soul
and get closer to the infinite and greater you.

Mastery Over Misery

Part of the mastery of life has to do with
the tailoring of your actions down to
only those that actually serve you.
Hold the space in your consciousness for
the concept of wellness in your daily life.
Eat better, sleep longer, give more,
think less, and love deeper.

Stories of Freedom

The reason stories of freedom are so compelling
to your heartstrings is that freedom is the song
your soul softly sings to you every blessed day.
Your soul seeks freedom in expression through the
physical experiences in your life and never leaves your side.
Your soul knows your life plan and guides you along your path.
What each soul knows is beyond the mind, beyond thought,
and beyond form. Your soul is the divine intelligence of
pure unbound consciousness in you.

This Moment Is All That Matters

Be careful to avoid drama in your life; the consequence is toxicity.
Don't become fascinated with your story to the degree that you tell it
over and over to anyone who will listen to you. Your story is interesting
and uniquely yours, but when you tell your story with an emphasis on
your past, it blocks the happiness available to you in the present moment.
If you define yourself by past circumstances, you will bypass today's joy.
Live for today and free yourself from the binding chains of yesterday.
This moment is all that matters; don't miss it.

Activating the Greater You

We are guided mostly by our minds,
which always act instinctively to protect our egos.
Instead of following your thoughts, try to follow
the intuition of your heart. Quiet your mind as you
dissolve into silent meditation and simply surrender
to the now. Submerge yourself into the full appreciation
of the present moment. When you allow your soul to
guide your movements, you will activate the awesome
power of the greater you.

Gaps in Your Progression

Your reality experience is constantly shifting, and it affects the
quality of your thoughts and emotions. Your soul's evolution can
be found in each and every divine moment of your existence.
In your progression toward higher consciousness, there will be
times when there seems to be no development at all, but don't
be discouraged. These gaps are built-in pauses in your spiritual
growth. Cellular division always occurs immediately following
a period of rest. These pauses are an opportunity to reflect on
your current position and redirect your focus. Revitalize your health
with good nutrition, sleep, meditation, exercise, and prayer. Position
yourself in nature as often as possible and hold appreciation for
the beautiful world you live in. Refresh your mind with positive
ideas and thoughts of gratitude. Share your gifts with those who
are less fortunate, and expect exponential growth over time.

There Is a Power in Your Touch

There is power contained in the human touch.
Touch triggers an exchange of energy from one being to another.
Touch can be used as an instrument to heal or hurt, to love or hate,
to encourage or discourage, to support or destroy. The truth is that
one's spirit can be lifted and healed by a simple and loving touch.

Free the Mind and Cure the Body

As a being of light, wellness naturally flows to you and through you.
Proper alignment of the mind, body, heart, and soul generates
feelings of happiness and joy. Disorders of the mind lead to
disorders of the body. When you harbor thought patterns of
resistance, such as fear and doubt, you block the flow of energy
through the meridians of your body. If you can remove the
resistance dampening your flow, the Source energy within
you can move more freely. Pure love and joy are all that remain.

And So It Begins

(Read aloud)
And so it begins.
The eyes are closed,
the mind is quiet,
the body is still,
the breath is calm,
the vision is inward,
the soul is centered,
the ego is lost,
the broken heart heals,
and the wounded spirit is mended.
Inhale—calm.
Exhale—ease.
Love is real.

CHAPTER 15

Universe

Trust the Universe

We all must trust that there is an all-knowing force that is stronger than we are. The limitless power surrounding us is Source: the Creator, or God. The universe consists of all existing matter and space; it arises from and persists through the grace of God. The universe is believed to have been formed more than thirteen billion years ago and contains a vast number of galaxies. We are made of this same cosmic energy, and, like the universe, we are constantly expanding and evolving. Everything in existence is filled with a supreme intelligence derived from Source. If we are one with the whole, then we are one with the Creator. All abundance flows from this unseen force, but if we don't trust it, that flow is cut off. The more we trust the universe, the more abundance flows into our lives.

Conflict

To be more trusting, we must remove the blocks in our consciousness that prevent us from believing in ourselves. If we see the world as a threatening place, we will be unable to enjoy all the beauty life has to offer. We each fight a battle within, an inner struggle against ourselves. This internal conflict interferes with our spiritual growth. To make significant progress, we must turn our attention inward and identify the issues that hinder our ideal vibration. We can find freedom through visualization and truth through light.

Individual Perspective and Position

The universe is full of stars that fill the night sky. From the perspective of each star, the universe appears different. There isn't one view that is superior to another. Each star's position is needed to balance the integrity of the cosmos. Likewise, as human beings, we are each unique and have different views of the world. Each position is independent and beautiful, forming a diverse set of beliefs, which all contribute to the fabric of our existence. When we respect the beliefs of others as much as we do our own, we usher in the power of oneness. Our levels of compassion, understanding, and love for one another accelerate our evolution as spiritual beings. The power of one man is strong, but the power of all mankind is infinite.

The universe loves you no matter what mistakes you make here on earth. The universe is constantly listening to you and supporting you. Put your worries aside and trust that the universe has your back. Call on the universe to take action on your behalf. You are the universe, but when you invite it to act on your behalf, your highest potential is activated. Your focus should be to elevate your consciousness and learn how to master your vibration. Always believe that you are deserving and will survive your challenges. Hope and faith create the way for your dreams to materialize. When you maintain faith in the order of things, God will bless you in ways beyond what you can even imagine.

As your disbelief dissipates, a knowing replaces your wanting. Know that everything happening to you is for your soul's evolution. The universe is constantly evolving and creating for you, so it helps to be unified with it and all of creation.

Trusting the Universe and Yourself

Trusting the universe isn't about letting go of everything in your life and hoping to be saved. It's about knowing you have a powerful connection with the stars, the cosmos, and everything around you. Your body is formed from the earth, and when your life is over, you shall return to the earth. Therefore, trusting the universe isn't about trusting something external to you but about trusting the same Source you were created from. There is a supreme force that created all that is before us; that force is the power of God. If we position ourselves as weak, disempowered, and disassociated in our relationship with God, and perceive the universe as somehow outside ourselves, then we are living a fantasy. The universe isn't separate from you; the universe is inside you. Knowing this truth creates a superpower called *faith*. Having faith is an inner knowing that you are derived from a power greater than yourself. The best way to trust the universe is to trust yourself. When you trust yourself, you become empowered with the same power that spins the earth on its axis and creates worlds beyond our galaxy.

In 1950, the German-born psychologist Erik Erikson labeled our first life lesson "trust versus mistrust." In the first year of life, a newborn's experience shapes the way they view the world for the rest of their life. The purpose of a newborn's cry is to expand their lungs and heart as well as to communicate their every need. If babies' cries are heard and promptly responded to, they develop a trusting bond and attachment with their caretaker. A secure attachment creates a loving trust of the baby's external world and fosters a feeling of safety, which builds inside the child throughout their life. If children feel supported, they will develop into well-adjusted adults, empowered to venture out into the world and explore new territories. When babies are born into scarcity, they often grow up to have a mistrust of people, society, and the world in general. This isn't to say that these children will grow up to be sociopaths; their experiences shape their overall view of the world and predispose them to develop a shortage of consciousness. Confidence and supreme security in oneself destroys inferior states of lack and indifference.

Your Outer Universe Creates Your Inner Universe

Stop blaming the messengers for your discomfort. They come with bad news to remind you that you are out of alignment with the universe. When you are aligned with the universe, there is no stress, and you are fully trusting in God's plan for you. By trusting the universe, you can modify your belief system to include a loving world and a supportive universe. "When you are happy, heaven rejoices," Diana Cooper once said. When you surrender to a power greater than yourself, you become better able to have intimate relationships, maintain an emotional balance, and rebound from disappointment and failure.

In summary, your outer universe is created from your inner universe. The universe rearranges itself to reflect the current condition of your mind. When we discover our real relationship with life, we lose all fear and insecurity, and we replace them with faith and knowingness. There is freedom in knowing. There is a key to unlocking this change of heart; the key is love. Love frees us from the chains of doubt and enables us to taste the spiritual tonic of God. The power of good is all around us, and faith in this power allows us to use it to rid ourselves of limitation and scarcity. Every man and woman was born with the gift of limitless freedom, and we are here to discover this truth. As we gain understanding of the subtle laws of nature, we will gradually be set free. The truth frees us to be joyful and prosperous in this amazing place we call the universe.

You Did Not Create Yourself

You did not create yourself. There is a power in the universe
that is greater than you. God is like an ocean that flows through us.
Inside each body runs a powerful river of energy that touches
every heart and stirs each soul. Each person's life expression is like
a fountain that sprays upward and outward as long as the channel
between God and our hearts remains unblocked and open.
Don't let your stuff get between you and the Creator.
Let your river run.

You Are a Highly Charged Spirit

You are a highly charged spirit that has ascended to earth to
take on the challenges of a sometimes unpredictable world.
Along your journey, you will encounter many storms because
you need their gifts. Your faith, dedication, and willpower will
all be tested. Your spirit will either grow or wither from these
very experiences. When you emerge from your struggles,
you will gain the strength and resilience you need to thrive
and survive. Your future ascension depends on your decisions
and deeds of today. Universal love is the luminous light cast
onto your path of expansion. Find the light and follow the love.

The Breath of God Gave You Life

When the crest of the earth shifts, it causes enormous seismic events
that create majestic mountains under the sea. Violent motion of
the earth's tectonic plates produces geological shifts in the ocean.
The sands of the ocean floor shift in a brilliant response, and beautiful
gigantic waves are born. Each wave has only one destiny: to crash
magnificently against the shore. When your spirit is being challenged
and your foundation is shaking, take comfort in knowing you have
greatness inside you. The infinite power of God and the ancient wisdom
of your soul sustain you. Everything that happens to you is happening
to awaken your inner truth. Each event in your life has a divine purpose.
The breath of God gave you life and gifted you with a soul destined to
carry out His will. May His will be done.

Millions of Realities

There is only one earth, but there are millions of realities. Each one of us lives in our own unique world. Everyone's worldly perspective is different and custom suited to match their existing beliefs. This individuality is the real magnificence of creation. Be delighted by its splendor and humbled by its existence.

The Universe Is Always Expanding

The universe is full of stars that fill the night sky. From the perspective of each star, the universe is different. There's not a single perspective that is superior to another. From any single point, beauty can be seen. Each star is magnificent all by itself, but each is only a small part of something much greater. What affects a single star is felt by the entire universe. Stars are born, and stars will die, but, the universe, like our inner space, is always expanding.

The Vital Life Force

The vital life force in all living things is the thread that connects us all. This dynamic universal field is full of pure vibrational potential. The universe is as big as our imaginations, and it is constantly expanding. It is omnipresent in all we see, feel, and experience. It is the background for our very existence. This divine vibrational field serves as the stage for the development and maturation of us all. History is the story of our lives through the lens of time. The intelligence of the universe is the genesis of creative ideas and the cradle of our dreams. This amazing divine intelligence is also known as Source.

The Universe Contains Boundless Love Intelligence

There is energy in nature.
If you're feeling drained, replenish your power by going outdoors.
Plants and trees radiate healing energy forces that are beneficial
to all mankind. Sense the warmth, brilliance, and light of this
amazing planet. Breathe in deeply and fill your inner being with
loving energy. Let your lungs expand with all the beauty that
you feel. The universe contains boundless love intelligence.
Love is energy, and energy is power. May the power of love
always be present in you.

The Cycles of the Sun and Moon

The majestic nature of our planet is revealed in our
beautiful sunrises and sunsets. The transition cycles of
the sun and moon stir a comparison to the spiritual
transformation happening inside all human beings.
As evolving souls, we all go through phases in our lives.
We love, we laugh, and sometimes we cry.
We rise, we shine, and sometimes we fall.
When we fall down, we must get back up again.
The cycle repeats itself, but the dawn of each day
and the setting of each sun forever changes us.

You Are the Universe

You and the universe are one. The great beyond of
outer space that physically surrounds you is also
a part of you. It is part of you, and you are part of it.
The universe, in all its splendor, is you. Behold,
the infinite wisdom of everything and everyone
who has ever lived is contained inside you.

Trust the Universe

Up ahead there is a divergent divide in your flow of consciousness. Around the bend there is a crossing where you will have to make an important choice. You can choose to continue swimming upstream and fight the current, or you can trust the universe, let go, and float downstream on your journey. When you allow the twists and turns of life to serve as turning points in your spiritual progression, you cannot help but pivot and grow. Which path you choose to follow determines everything else in your life.

There Is No Book of Life

There is no book of life.
The information you have been told is full of untruths.
But don't panic; there's no need for concern. Those perpetuating this scenario did so thinking they were protecting you from an unkind world. You were led to believe this world is a kind place, but, instead, it can sometimes be a harsh reality. You were sold a love story, but love can be a jungle. You were filled with dreams of having a big, happy family, but raising a family is the most challenging thing you will ever do. You were promised longevity, but tomorrow isn't promised to anyone. In spite of all this, you are blessed with the gift of creativity and invention. You are only limited by the boundaries of your imagination. Nothing in life is guaranteed, but all things are possible.

You Graduate This Level of Consciousness

You graduate this level of consciousness by mastering the ability to deliberately create your reality. The key is to understand you have the power to control the way you feel regardless of your circumstances. If you can remain neutral to what you are seeing, you can attach the feeling you prefer to any experience. This skill set enhances your self-control and facilitates your ascension to deeper levels of consciousness.

CHAPTER 16

Transformation

The Metamorphosis of Oneself

Spiritual and physical evolution is the natural course of all mankind. Man has evolved physically, intellectually, and spiritually since humans first set foot on earth. A divine plan of evolution is already in place and is working for you and for all humanity. A new world order is being established where love rules. The next step in our evolution is the mass movement of human consciousness away from the limitations of fear, violence, and struggle, and toward freedom, harmony, and oneness. This process not only serves us as people but also ultimately serves a role in the salvation of planet earth. The earth is weakening as a result of centuries of use and abuse at the hands of greed. The polar ice caps are diminishing, the Amazon rain forests are being stripped, the greed of capitalism is draining the earth of its oil resources, many animal species are becoming extinct, and global warming is threatening the future existence of generations to come. Worldwide conflict is spreading, and oppressive governments and terrorism are turning some countries into refugee camps. The politics of fear and lies have overturned the impact of decades of civil rights marches and laws made to protect the rights of the oppressed. In the United States, silence and passivity have replaced the screams for equality. Once again, our society has turned a blind eye to the victims of poverty. In order to deliver the right cure to this nation and to the planet, we must unite and align with the soul of planet earth. The planet is in need of a global healing. Mahatma Gandhi once said, "Be the change you wish to see in the world." It's all about your inner journey and the outer sharing of your wisdom and grace. Healing the planet starts with healing your own suffering. Your spiritual awakening is your contribution to the healing of our planet. This worldwide crisis is in our hands. It's up to you, me, and the billions of people of this planet to shift to a higher state of consciousness. This global shift toward enlightenment is already under way. Many souls are being awakened at his very moment. Will you stand aside and watch this awakening, or will you answer the call and be a part of the solution?

Choice versus Freedom

Many people have the power of choice, but they are not free. In my recent trip to Cuba, I spoke to many people who felt the pressure of Communist rule. They longed for fair wages, lower taxes, and greater representation. The people I spoke to desired to fully express their workmanship and creativity, but they didn't have the opportunity for expression. Repression from governments, churches, or states can't suppress the real you. Freedom begins the moment you surrender to whatever is happening in the moment and understand that your soul is already free. Your soul can never be repressed because it is nonphysical and everlasting. No matter where you are, the realization that you have always been unbound and free at the level of your soul brings the sense of liberation.

The Spiritual Journey

The spiritual journey is the way in which a person awakens to their inner essence and finds God consciousness in themselves. At the heart of this metamorphosis is a shift away from a mind-made personal identity to that of an awakened spiritual being. The sounds you hear stirring deep down in your soul are those of a spiritual revolution. This transformational shift moves human beings up the ladder of consciousness. As each being awakens to their true nature, they learn to see life through the eye of their soul. "The soul is the perceiver and revealer of truth," Emerson once said. Discovering one's divine essence dissolves all fear and pain, ushering in the light of truth and love.

Choosing Transformation

We are all on the journey of self-realization, but many people do not complete the journey in their lifetime because it remains buried deep in their subconscious. People spend many years going through high school and college, perhaps studying to become a doctor or a lawyer; and yet, how many days does one spend with the intention to bring about change in oneself? The choice everyone must make is this: to continue to awaken unconsciously, or to begin to seek an awakening consciously. The journey of awakening is calling for your conscious participation.

In the eyes of most people, working hard and playing hard are enough to satisfy the urges of their ego. Most people resist change by remaining consistent in their routines, behaviors, and rituals. Everyone knows somebody who buys their cup of coffee at the same coffee shop every morning, then takes the same route to work, speaks to the same people, watches the same television shows, and goes to bed at the same time every night. And then the person repeats the same routine every day of the week while wishing and hoping their life will somehow change. Change cannot happen in your life until you decide to seek it. The addition of spirituality in your life is a choice. The magical turning point in transformation is when you stop paying attention to your mind and ask yourself how love would handle your current situation. This pivotal awareness shifts your vibration into the higher frequency of heart-based consciousness. Living life without a sense of spirituality is like driving a car without a steering wheel.

Your inner river of energy always flows downstream. When you encounter resistance and find yourself in a crisis, you are paddling upstream. At that point, changing your direction is advisable. Your highest flow state is always downstream. In fact, everything you want is located downstream; this is the direction of Source. Life in personhood surely has its moments, but the ego has no limits to its wants and desires. The more money, power, or fame you attain, the ego will still be unsatisfied and always want more. Many people lose their lives every day in search of ego gratification. If a person can change their inner concepts and beliefs, their whole life can change for the better.

Spiritual transformation requires a desire for change. Everyone must ask themselves, is it possible for me to get more out of life? You must be willing to give up who you are for what you can become. The daily mantra I repeat every morning is "I am choosing to grow. God, allow me be a better person today than I was yesterday. I will no longer consciously contribute to my own distraction from who I really am and why I am here." The day you throw yourself completely open and surrender to a power higher than yourself is the day you will become liberated and truly free. Transformation is the shift of consciousness toward the inner self. Once a person's balance point between their inner and outer self shifts inward, transformation is inevitable. According to Dr. Wayne Dyer, "Transformation literally means going beyond your form." How you taste existence is based on your thoughts, emotions, and memories. Ram Dass states, "One way to understand spiritual work within an individual incarnation is to see it as a shift from identifying with your mind to identifying with your soul." Transformation is indeed a metamorphosis of oneself. As we shift our vibrational energy to the state of love, there are innumerable changes that occur in the body, mind, and heart.

Signs of Transformation

Signs you may be undergoing a shift in your life include the following: the world as it is stops making sense, you become restless and discontent with the way things are, painful emotions from your past come to the surface, and you desire to spend more time alone in meditation and reflection. You may suddenly develop the impulse to change jobs or even careers. You begin to spend more time living in the now, and you start to notice more coincidental meetings with people who were on your mind. As your transformation nears completion, you become a more compassionate, grateful, kind, and loving person. You will begin to recognize the efforts of some to divide our society. You become more intolerant of racism, conflict, and separation. When you live your life from your center, you become more focused, more resilient, more loving, mentally stronger, and divinely guided. Once your identity shifts to your soul, your reality will follow suit. From your new altitude, you will be able to accomplish feats that have always seemed improbable. With a higher consciousness, the impossible suddenly becomes possible.

Moving from Your Comfort Zone to Your Transformation Zone

We often build walls around ourselves in our pursuit of comfort and security. I often visualize people with a giant bubble of protection around them. This safety zone offers protection from the outside world, but it also limits personal growth. I urge you to question the very shelter in which you are taking refuge, and venture outside your comfort zone. As long as you remain in the shadows of comfort, you will miss out on the aliveness of life. The eternal movement of life is where the action is. There is little to no risk staying inside your bubble. Venturing out of your comfort zone adds risk, but it also increases your odds of success in life. Make the decision to push against the walls of your bubble to expand it. When you are stretching yourself, there will always be initial discomfort. Suffering is unavoidable in life. Out of suffering comes understanding and wisdom. Don't be afraid of the open sea of life; deep water is where the treasure lies.

What I call the transformation zone, or T-zone, is located just beyond your comfort zone, at the edge of your fears. You must learn to go past your points of fear or you will miss out on many of life's more delicious experiences. Your T-zone is the space in you where the only constant is change. This is your area for development and growth. Your T-zone is your launching pad into new experiences and adventures. This is where you must take your leaps of faith in this life. No risk, no gain. Be courageous. Trust your intuition to make daring choices when necessary. Maintain the belief that life is always working for you, not against you.

Awakening the Giant Within

Following your transformational shift, your rewired mind can avoid old triggers that once led you into struggle and conflict. The process of awakening cleanses the mind and energizes the soul. As you get more comfortable living from your center, you become more balanced and productive. Connecting with your higher self now happens easily when called upon. The idea of going back to old sticky thought patterns of the past becomes unwanted and even repulsive. A new boost of awareness takes place in your consciousness, and your evolution into an enlightened being begins to take shape. Because of spiritual transformation, you arrive at a state of being that is free of the constraints of the past and open to progressive changes of the future. You gain a new perspective on past dramas and behavioral patterns in your life.

The Fire of Transformation

Transformation is analogous to a fire that burns away aspects of your being that you no longer need. Forest fires are an aspect of nature. Through the inferno, life emerges because the heat is necessary to free seeds from pine cones of a certain species of pine tree. Fire burns away underbrush and clears the ground for new growth. The burning of our outer shell hurts in many ways, but what remains unburned after the fire is our inner shell, the part of us that is nonphysical and everlasting. Your transformation happens from the inside out. There's a fire burning inside each of us: the fire of transformation. Some of us smell smoke, and others don't. Some of us are on fire, and some of us are not. Some of us are willing to burn, and others are unwilling to learn. The spiritual benefits from your inner fire is liberation from incessant thinking and your emotional attachments. Beyond your thoughts and feelings lies your soul. This epic transformational shift in you is accompanied by an enhanced sense of awareness and an absence of judgment. Your new perspective is from the seat of your soul, and the position of the unchanging watcher of your experience. Debbie Ford says, "Your outer shell serves to protect you from the world while your real treasure, your soul's expression, is hidden within." At some point in your life, there must be a curiosity that leads to the meticulous study of your deep consciousness and true nature. Divine transformation awakens the giant within you and has many benefits for your body mind as well. As you begin to live at the level of the self, you live more consciously and lovingly.

Pure Loving Awareness

Spreading love and oneness is the natural effect of the spiritual journey. An awakened soul has peace in their heart and a deep and profound love for all beings and all things. The fresh scent of forgiveness is omnipresent. The enlightened one is nonjudgmental and sees everything in the universe as unfolding. As the witness of your experience, you aren't easily moved by life events and stay neutral to the happenings in the world. In an enlightened state, form and formless become one, held together by the supreme force of unconditional love. In your life, you are always returning home to your loving truth: oneness with God.

All that is currently unconscious about you will eventually be brought into the light of consciousness. This awakened divinity in you is your true nature. This spiritual process is known as *self-realization,* the state of knowing that who you are is pure loving awareness. This boost of consciousness is transmuted into light itself. This new state is known as *presence,* which is the realm of the timeless and formless, your true identity beyond name and form. As presence, you become a bridge between God and the world.

A New Perspective on Death

A new outlook on death and dying also accompanies the journey of awakening. Many philosophers have attributed the fear of death as the primary moving force behind people's thoughts, behaviors, and actions. In self-realization, knowing that you are an eternal being replaces the fear of death. With your new elevated state of awareness, you live life louder and also with a profound sense of purpose. As realized beings, we begin to see that death isn't the end but a new beginning in the spiritual world. People don't really die; they are simply released into another form. Discovering the truth of your being is liberating. The gift of freedom from your body mind marks the end of seeing your death as a finite ending to your journey.

Most people associate death with the loss of the life force when, actually, the opposite is true. In death, your attachment to your body mind is broken. Your soul is released from its contract with your body, and is reunited with God. Attachment is the root cause of all suffering. When you die, it is actually your attachments that die. Death is an illusion and is better described as a rebirth into the spiritual world. "That which is born of the flesh is flesh; and that which is born of the Spirit is spirit" (John 3:6). In death, there is no disconnection from your being; death is just a transition to another dimension. In your ultimate transition, your soul will feel as if you are waking up from a dream and walking into your true reality. This is because physical reality on earth is very limiting, while spiritual reality is much more expansive. We are consciousness experiencing itself subjectively, and there is no such thing as death.

Before You Were Born

Before you were born, you were formless and nameless. After your birth, you were given a name and formed an identity from your mind and body. In death, you simply surrender your body back to earth and return to your original formless state. Your heavenly ascension signifies your freedom from suffering in the physical realm and also celebrates the release of the physical limitations of your body. "Life is only a dream and we are the imagination of ourselves," Bill Hicks once said.

Death is like peeling a banana: when the body is peeled back, the naked soul is exposed. Truthfully, death isn't darkness but ascension into light. What I am pointing to is the journey in which our souls go to heaven to be with God. This heaven isn't the one filled with angels gathered at the pearly gates. Instead, it is an intangible heaven in a timeless dimension adorned by the waiting arms of God.

Transformation Is a Painful Process

When a seed is planted in the rich black soil of the earth, it is submerged in darkness. Through blind faith and courage, that seed grows and eventually breaks through the darkness of the ground to emerge into the sunlight. Finally free to thrive and reach its potential, that once-tiny seed transforms into a beautiful flower. Likewise, by blind faith and determination, you will also emerge from your dark situation. Transformation is a painful process, but it is easier when you are armed with the belief that nothing can stop you from evolving into light.

This Journey Spares No One

If everything in your life was always wonderful, there would be no internal suffering. Without suffering, there would be no reason to turn inward toward self-realization. There is no greater place to experience this process other than life itself. Our earthly existence is really about the gradual process of your transformation into love and light. To learn, you must sometimes fail; to transform, you must endure suffering. In the very end, you will die to make the final transition into everlasting light. This journey calls everyone and spares no one.

Clarity Always Arrives at the End

It doesn't matter whether you fully understand what is happening in your life right now or not. Fear is the source of all anxiety and confusion. The key to an abundant life is to trust your journey and allow your transformation to happen spontaneously and organically. When you relax, your situation becomes more flexible. Face tomorrow with great courage and faith. Open your mind to the presence of limitless possibilities. Remain mindful that there is a natural flow to your evolution. When your circumstances become challenging, keep the faith that you will reach your most favorable outcomes. Clarity is never present in the beginning of any journey; clarity always arrives at the end.

You Are Not the Body Mind

When medical illness strikes you, such as hypertension, diabetes, or cancer, remember that you are not the body. Likewise, remember that you are not the mind. You aren't a physical being having a spiritual experience; you are a spiritual presence having an earthly experience. You have the choice to see yourself as spirit, and, thus, no physical disease or condition can ever define your earthly existence. May this give you the strength and power to overcome your current health crisis. Don't ever forget where you came from. Your spiritual energy is derived directly from Source. By this light, you can tolerate and overcome any negative health issues you may be facing. And so it is.

The Supreme

Relax and release the anxiety behind your current situation. Use the challenges in your life as an opportunity to access your higher self. Transformation is always a painful process. Remember that parts of you must die for you to be reborn. Every action you take is in avoidance of your inevitable death. Facing your greatest fear frees you and places you into alignment with your greatest truth. There is no separation between you and the Supreme.

Your Life

Your life is about your discipline.
Your discipline is about your commitment.
Your commitment is your purpose.
Your purpose is to evolve.
When we evolve, we transform into love.

I Want to Burn Like a Meteor

I want to burn like a meteor, rocketing upward and outbound:
accelerating, shining brightly, and being absolutely fearless.
I want to leave behind a trail of fire and space dust from
here to infinity. I desire to be free of all limitations of time and space.
My aim is just beyond the horizon, and at the end of my journey
I will break into countless tiny particles of pure divine love.

Shattered by My Transition

Shattered by my transition on earth,
I broke into a trillion tiny pieces.
I smelled the dust of humanity as
I disintegrated into nothingness.
As I relaxed and let go of my former self,
the dark abyss beyond the horizon
slowly revealed itself.
I floated with clarity and purpose into
the great and infinite realm beyond.
I became weightless as the particles of
my former body dissipated into outer space.
Although I was separating from
everything I had ever known,
I felt true joy and a sense of liberation.
I heard a thousand thunders.
I saw an aurora for the first time.
I experienced unbelievable revelations.
Higher consciousness was my deliverance,
and in one brief moment, I was reborn.

Death Is a Myth

Death is a myth.
You cannot ever really die.
No part of the real you experiences death.
Your soul merely transitions into spirit consciousness:
pure grace and light beyond the stratosphere and
into another time and another dimension.

I Am Ready for My Transformation

(Read aloud)
I am ready for my transformation.
I cannot resist this change any longer.
I am willing to separate from what
I know for certain, and surrender
to the unfamiliar and the unknown.
If forgiveness comes calling, I will forgive.
If free fall is the task, I am willing to let go.
If suffering is the price, I am willing to pay.
If the fire is the test, I am willing to burn.
If love is the answer, I must ask the question:
who am I—man or spirit?

CHAPTER 17

True Self versus the Ego

Residing in Your True Nature

Ego Development

In the womb, a baby experiences an oceanic sense of oneness through its connection to the mother. This occurs in the form of the umbilical cord and placenta, which physically unite the two. When a baby is born, the cord is cut, the placenta is discarded, and the baby becomes an entity by itself. A baby's first stage of life is marked by its struggle to survive. Early on, the infant depends on its mother's milk and the love and attention of its primary caretakers. This period builds trust in the mind of the baby and marks the beginning of the formation of its personality, individuality, and independence.

A baby naturally develops its ego very early in life. This is the awakening sense that "I am not my mother" and "I am a unique self." The ego is an essential part of each of us. The soul creates the ego so that it can experience itself in the physical world. Without a healthy ego, we cannot be independent or reach our greatest potential. A child has difficulty understanding life from any perspective other than its own. In this time frame, children are very "me, myself and I" oriented. It isn't unusual for a young child to believe the world is created for them and that they can control it. At around eleven or twelve years old, a child can think abstractly, but thoughts are still mostly egocentric. Adolescence is a period characterized by biological, hormonal, cognitive, and social changes. Puberty is a time of rapid growth toward responsibility and independence. Adolescent autonomy is strongly related to ego development and self-esteem. The function of the ego, according to Loevinger (1976), is to create a frame of reference from which an individual's inner experiences and perception of external events can be understood. The ego believes everything it does, and everything it is, results from its own actions. The ego sees itself as separate from all other beings, but in reality, it is not.

Actions of the Ego

It's important to have a healthy ego. A robust ego has a sense of what our interests, talents, and work have made us. While a thriving ego is necessary to survive in our sophisticated world, the greatest opportunity of the human experience is to expose the lie that we are merely a personality with a body. The greatest discovery in the journey of self-realization is that we are consciousness itself and not just people. The ego is just a small piece of our true nature, which is the self. In personhood, there is always a void that seeks something more in life, but the ego blocks us from finding the source of this void by always turning our consciousness outward. It tries to alleviate our inner pain by feeding us with outside energies of admiration, attention, and power. In one ear, the ego whispers, "You are great!" In the other ear, it whispers, "You deserve better." Thus, you are never satisfied where you are. There seems to be no limit to the cravings of the ego. You diminish the ego by seeking its identity. Once you become aware of the boundaries of your ego, it begins to dissolve, and then it can no longer be all of who you are. Your awareness is a powerful tool for change and awakening.

Wanting and Craving

The five senses of the body mind are what the soul uses to experience this world. We must analyze the craving for the gratification of the five senses. Without transcending this ever-present wanting and craving, there can be no inner peace. It is this insatiability, and the attachment to it, which ultimately ends in conflict and misery. Freedom from craving is called *virtue,* which adds strength to the self. It is only by our awareness and alignment with our higher selves that we are able to transcend our limitations in this world of form. For most individuals, the distraction and intoxication of these outside energies keep them in personhood their whole lives. Billions of souls have passed through this journey we call life without ever realizing and activating the presence and power of their higher self. Don't waste your time here on earth; your awakening is possible for you in this lifetime.

Suffering and Conflict

Much of the discomfort you experience in life is because you are tired of suffering in your identity as a person. Facing the truth is not easy, because most people choose stability over freedom. They hang on to what they feel confident about, and they resist change. When you stand in opposition to change, it creates pressure and resistance against the natural flow of the universe. People who remain standing in opposition to change attract suffering. Those who accept change are constantly growing and evolving; they are no longer in opposition to life.

At this primal stage, your relationship with God is marked by feelings of separation. The longing is valid because God is calling you home. Somewhere inside each human being, a part of the person is seeking freedom toward a limitless expansion, but identity with the physical body is quite limiting. Releasing one's identification with the body mind frees the soul.

A complete identification with one's thoughts constructs an identity known as the *mind-made self.* This story-based identity is also called *the story of me.* Such people identify with and are fascinated by mental formations. In the world of form, there is a fascination with people, places, and things, but there is a contraction of one's inner space.

Complaining is a significant part of what sustains this limited identity. Take away the person's problems and complaints, and there is little left. Complaints draw contrast between ourselves and others. The action itself diminishes someone or something, and thus temporarily elevates the ego of the complainer.

Conflict and War

Conflict is another tool of the ego. In conflict, there is a need to declare a winner and a loser. This competition for energy enhances the ego of the aggressor and reduces that of the victim. The ego seeks conflict to further boost itself and aims to defeat outside competition. This is the basis of both individual conflict and war. War is the result of conflict to inflate the confidence of an entire tribe or nation. War offers little gain in terms of solutions and is very costly to the spiritual consciousness and energy of the participants. Despite the ghastly effects of thousands of years of conflict and war, which have only resulted in more suffering, we as a society have thus far been unable to break this painful cycle. There can only be peace in the world when the intense craving for dominant power can be recognized, understood, and transcended. It is the ego that has created wars and the tools of war. The justification for going to war is often the elimination of evil and injustice. However, by fighting evil, the individual or nation becomes the evil which they are seeking to eliminate. The transformation out of this vicious cycle does not lie with the formation of new alliances between nations but in the transformation of the individual consciousness of each human. The solution always lies outside the problem. In the case of war, conflict will always have a presence in the world until we surrender to peace. We must each surrender ourselves individually until the world as a whole unites in oneness and universal love. Spread love, not war.

Self-Realization

Once the desire for self-realization arrives and you become aware of your ties to ego-based consciousness, your spiritual journey is well under way. Eastern and Western gurus all quote the old saying "You must be a light unto yourself." Don't follow anybody; you have to go beyond yourself. The current of consciousness is always carrying you. All you must do is let go of the patterns of resistance holding you back. Once you begin this magnificent journey, there is no turning back. Thought by thought, action by action, the spiritual journey takes you on a one-way trip home.

At the level of the self, there is no heaven or hell; no religion can claim this level, and it is a place where there is no fear. It is a timeless and dimensionless space beyond form and name. The self has no identity, no thought, and no story behind it. All stories are told from the identity of a person, and so they keep the storyteller trapped in the dimension of time, space, and physical reality.

When you shift your identity to the "I Amness," nothing is missing. You begin to see yourself as complete. There are no more illusions or delusions, no intentions, anxiety, depression, or disease. The self is neither young nor old; it is neither rich nor poor; it is birthless and deathless. To know and be the self is the greatest discovery imaginable. You are the one who controls the breath. You are the absolute, the one who remains in the realm of silence and grace. The one who is here, but was never born. Beingness is the great inner space of God realization. You may surrender your identity of personhood to the self. The self is felt by the body, but the body cannot live in it.

When you honor this divinity in yourself, love, peace, wisdom, and joy arise in you. This is the dawn of a new heart-based consciousness motivated by the fragrance of love and freedom emitted from the escape from your overactive mind. As you deplete yourself of personal identity and empty yourself of all desires, intentions, and attachments, surrender is your constant companion. When you discover the truth of who you really are, your light is absolutely revealed, and you awaken to the realization that you are not the body mind; you are consciousness itself. Know this truth to be yourself. Relax in its splendor, for you have discovered the dimension of the greater you.

The Path of Your True Self

When you are evolving, you are on the path of growing and
thereby following your true self. When you are static, you are
not growing, and you are following the way of your false self.
Anytime you're less than your authentic self, you are
creating and starring in an illusion in a parallel reality.
No progression of consciousness can happen in the illusion,
only along the path of your true self. When you show up as
less than authentic in the world, your outcomes become
much less favorable. On the other hand, when you are
being authentic, the world responds accordingly with
a measured dose of blessings and love.

You Are a Radiant Being

Don't try to be someone other than your true self;
this will only delay your spiritual journey. When you live
each day authentically, your awakening will accelerate with
great speed. Everything you need to thrive and build
on is available to you in the present moment. When you
awaken to your truth, you walk into your divine light. You are
a radiant being. May your inner light shine brightly and be a
source of inspiration to all those whose lives you touch.

Be the Light

Every scenario contains the infinite genius and
mighty power of positivity, which always offsets
the presence of any amount of negativity that
may be building around you. Love is always
surrounding you and protecting you. Don't just
see the light in the world; be the light.
The real you is the light of your very soul.

Your Enlightened Inner Being

Have you ever noticed how friends often perceive a change in you before you discover the change yourself? This is a subtle measurement of your disconnect with your higher mind. We are so busy hiding behind our makeup, clothing, and masks, that we are unable to see the changes that have already happened in our spiritual evolution. Your inner power always reflects outward. This is your personal aura that other human beings see, sense, and feel. It's time for the greater you to emerge. When you close the gap between your true self and your false self, you are able to better reflect the limitless power of your enlightened inner being.

Remain in the Stillness

Don't trust your thoughts or emotions; they are just like clouds passing by. Let them pass. More thoughts will come and go. Let them pass too. Thoughts have no power until you add your attention and belief to them. Remain in the stillness of pure loving awareness. Consciousness is like an ocean. The waves we see on the surface of the ocean constitute only a small fraction of the total depth of the whole. Likewise, your thoughts and emotions are just a small fraction of who you really are as your complete nonphysical self.

Judgment

When we judge others and their actions, we can see exactly what they're doing wrong. Furthermore, we believe we know exactly what they need to do to fix their problems. We are far better at judging others than ourselves because we see ourselves as separate from other people. Once we begin to see humanity as one united spirit, inner consciousness expands, and our own issues reveal themselves more clearly.

The Voice Inside Your Head

What is the voice inside your head telling you?
Is that voice saying positive or negative things to you?
Who is speaking? How does this conversation make you feel?
Learn to identify the voice of your higher mind, which is
always positive and encouraging. The ego mind at times
makes you feel less than you truly are. Aligning yourself
with your truth always feels great. Your true self is your
loving spirit that dances joyfully in the light.

In Tomorrow Lies a Promise

With the same certainty as the rising sun,
we are committed to the discovery of our true selves.
As we remove layer upon layer of misinformation and
false beliefs, we draw closer to our divine nature.
Although progression is sometimes slow, it is by our
unrelenting faith and willpower that we will ultimately
discover our truth and purpose. In tomorrow lies the
promise of a new day, where love replaces fear
and light replaces darkness.

The Final Mystery Is Oneself

The final mystery is oneself.
After you have climbed the highest mountains,
after you have sailed the roughest seas,
after you have journeyed to the most-exotic places,
the discovery of your true self still remains.
The adventure of the greater you awaits.
Your soul is always signaling for your attention.
All you must do is follow the whisper of your
inner voice. Your soul knows the way home.

CHAPTER 18

Oneness

Merging into Oneness

From the moment of your birth, the human condition creates an illusion of separation from the Creator. One of the great missions of life is to break the illusory glass of separation between your body mind and God. God isn't to be worshiped, feared, or understood, but, rather, to be experienced and known. The key to uniting with the Creator is to first discover unity within yourself. Your ego sees your existence in a fragmented state composed of a separate mind, body, heart, and soul. The truth is that all aspects of you are one whole entity. Fragmentation is brought about by your thoughts and beliefs about yourself.

Fragmentation versus Wholeness

The ego fights to retain fragmentation because, if you were ever able to unify all aspects of your consciousness, there would be little need or purpose for the existence of your ego. Your fragmentation can be observed at the level of the self, and if you can observe it, then you can separate from it, and it shall dissolve. When the fragmented aspects of you are one, you see the world from the higher perspective of the unified self. As these energies stabilize, you are able to view your life circumstances from the vantage point of balance and peace. Balance in life is achieved by centering yourself at the level of the soul. The wisdom and love of the self are infinite and offer clarity where there once was doubt. Living at the soul level allows no separation because of race, cultures, philosophies, and religions. The definition of oneness is to live in peace and harmony with all. Separation is just an illusion; everything is already one.

When you call yourself an Indian or a Muslim or a Christian
or a European, or anything else, you are being violent.
Do you see why it is violent? Because you are separating
yourself from the rest of mankind. When you separate yourself
by belief, by nationality, by tradition, it breeds violence.
So a man who is seeking to understand violence does not belong to
any country, to any religion, to any
political party or partial system;
he is concerned with the total understanding of mankind.

—Jiddu Krishnamurti

Transcending Separation

You are a multidimensional being. Until you can free yourself from the repetitive thought patterns limiting your ascension, you will always feel stuck in your experience. Once you increase your awareness, you can raise your vibration to a state where your higher self can be fully integrated into your consciousness. Moving your attention away from your incessant thought stream to your loving heart space creates a shift to a reality supported by nonjudgment, surrender, peace, and unconditional love. Once you find oneness in your life, you can easily feel the overwhelming support of the universe. From this sacred space, trust is ever present, and letting go of your shortage consciousness becomes easy. As your higher self, you are able to go beyond the limitations of your five physical senses and rise above the illusion of separation from God. Your new objective becomes staying as the self and seeing all your earthly experiences as opportunities to achieve harmony and oneness in yourself and the world.

As you begin to integrate the outer aspects of your being beyond your current level of understanding, oneness is no longer perceived as the end result of your spiritual journey but, rather, the beginning of a new level of existence. From your new perspective of oneness, you are able to break old thought patterns that created unwanted outcomes and begin to attract energies and circumstances that match your highest vibrational state. The moment you believe that you are the cocreator of your reality, instant manifestation becomes more prevalent. The time between a thought and that thought's manifestation into your reality is shortened, and you become a master of your life.

You are a piece of divine essence, and creation and free will are your gifts. From this new perspective, your ego and its desires no longer guide you. Your guidance from this point forward is by the divine force of God. It is as if your perspective of the world is elevated to the view from a mountaintop. Higher states of being, such as intuition, heightened awareness, and bliss, become yours. Your life will always reflect your current level of consciousness. As your consciousness expands, so does the quality of your experience.

Healing Division and Fragmentation

As a physician and scientist, I have studied the infrastructure of the human body and mind for nearly three decades. The background of our bodies is a delicate electrochemical system that controls the function of our internal organs and our minds. Typically, our five senses relay information from our bodies to our souls. Consider the state of oneness as a rewiring of your mind away from the dependency of your five senses and toward another dimension beyond form and into the realm of knowingness. Knowing is superior to thought and belief. You achieve the state of knowing by unifying with the God force inside you. In oneness, significant changes take place at your cellular level and return you to your original essence. This return to your natural state is a liberation from the body mind and its physical limitations. You are no longer bound to old paradigms. The realization of oneness is achieved by far fewer souls than those who search for it. The ones who become aligned with oneness must surrender to the One, only to realize that there wasn't any journey at all. We always were a child of the One. You are a miraculous, partly physical, mostly nonphysical, manifestation of the Divine. Your mission here on earth is to return to Source as the fully realized self; all rivers eventually flow back into the ocean.

From this free state of being, it is possible to explore your limitless self. All that is required to initiate this discovery is a desire for truth. The key is to trust the universe, and the way is the path of least resistance. The mind-set is knowing that no matter what your current circumstances are, your transformation to awakening is absolutely inevitable. Oneness is achieved by overcoming the forces that act to separate mankind into isolated pockets of humanity. Oneness speaks to building bridges between the body mind and the soul, men and women, philosophies and religions, nations and cultures, black and white, brown and yellow, us and them, and God and us.

Your Gift Is Your Soul

When you bare your soul to someone, you are
giving and sharing aspects of your inner essence.
What is deep inside you is pure love everlasting.
Sharing your incredible gift is inherently blissful.
The spell of your true self is both magnetic and
irresistible. Don't allow your fears of failing or
being rejected to ever conquer your dreams.
Your blessing is your gift. Your gift is your soul.

Begin to Sense and Feel Oneness

Begin to sense and feel oneness.
Close the separation between your mind, body, heart, and soul.
Peace is the place that exists in the harmony of oneness.
Silently explore the expansiveness of your soul. The universe
contains all you are and all that has ever mattered.
Glory to the goodness and essence of your being.

You Are a Miracle

I have attended thousands of births.
At each birth I have witnessed, a miracle took place.
Birth is the initial union of the mind, body, and soul.
I have seen the spirit of joy emerge from incapacitating pain, and
I have seen the misery of suffering turn into hysterical laughter.
Whenever the miracle of birth takes place, a baby's first breath
connects them to life in this realm. Another piece is added to
the universal puzzle, and all in the world is as it should be.
You have been a miracle since the day you were born.

Everyone in Your Life Has a Purpose

When you first meet another person, try not to judge them right away. The ultimate purpose of the people you meet in your life is seldom revealed from the start. The roles of your friends always evolve, and their purpose in your life will become more apparent to you over time. The space you hold for someone is the only space they can ever occupy. It is very tempting to judge people initially, but it is far more beneficial to patiently observe and allow your relationships to unfold over time. There are no wasted experiences in life. Everything and everyone in your life has a divine purpose. The very people we need the most are already right there in front of us.

There Is a Mission in Progress

There is a mission in progress we must join. Our highest mission is what calls all souls to unite as one. Come one, come all, and resist the temptation of separateness; it is a mind trap. Say yes to unity and no to divisiveness. The fragmented self is merely an illusion. When we stand together, we can elevate our collective consciousness to unimaginable levels and push the evolution of the human race toward oneness and universal love.

Vulnerability Is Not a Weakness

The key to maintaining a successful relationship is maintaining excellent lines of communication and exploring deeper states of vulnerability in one another. Vulnerability isn't a weakness; it is a door that love walks through. When you surrender to love, you open your sacred heart space. Authentic partnerships share a common intention to love harder and deeper, no matter what the circumstances are. The energetic forces that true love triggers in your heart last forever. There is always new territory to discover when true love reigns. When relationships fail, it is only because we wish them to. Humble yourself often; it takes two to win in the game of love. Don't try to control the process; love cannot be guided. Love must find its own way through the depths of your heart.

The Eyes Are the Window to the Soul

The eyes are indeed the window to the soul. When you are trying to connect with someone spiritually, look them directly in the eyes. Look inside them to experience the magnificent beauty of the person's inner light. Take a deep breath in, relax your posture, and smile. See inside other beings what you see in yourself. We are all interconnected by a universal energy field. Love has a gravitational pull in the universe, and love's energy is capable of being transferred across time and space at a velocity far beyond the speed of light. Feel the delightful exchange of connectivity between you and each soul you encounter. Develop your power of awareness to sense someone's distinct energy pattern and tune in to their signature frequency. Listen with your heart instead of your mind. We are here to connect with one another, to merge into oneness, and to love as deep as humanly possible.

There Is Only One You

There is something different about you. You don't remind me of anyone else. You have a unique vibration and frequency. No matter what you do, there is no one who does it quite like you. Your style is like no other. Your smile is radiant and special. Your grace is incomparable. Your loving heart is so expansive that it just may burst. Your creativity boggles my mind. I have met a lot of people in my life, but I have never met anyone quite like you. You are most definitely one of a kind. There is only one you.

The Diary of a Vibrational Mismatch

Sometimes, when you meet or greet someone, that person may not match your level of enthusiasm. You sense it instantly and feel uncomfortable. In these instances, you are detecting a vibrational discord, and it is best to move on. Everyone has a distinct vibrational frequency that reflects their internal energy. Some souls are just not your vibrational match. There is seldom any gain by staying in these interactions. Your intuition is detecting a resistance toward you or a significant misalignment of the other person. This type of encounter can also represent a competition for your energy. We always have a choice to use our energy to expand universal love or to reduce another soul. What type of vibration are you transmitting today?

CHAPTER 19

Awakening

The Journey of Awakening

Congratulations! Now that you have come to the end of this book, you are feeling quite different and empowered as compared to when you first started reading it. By now you have increased your awareness of the thoughts you are choosing to believe. You are choosing to put momentum behind only positive ideas and choices that make you feel good. You have become a more powerful spirit because you have rewired your mind to work for you instead of against you. Your positive mental attitude has provided you with a higher altitude to view your unique world. You now understand that your thoughts determine your vibration and how you feel. Your thoughts, beliefs, memories, and perspective manifest the world you see before you.

The truth is that, deep within, we are consciousness without the identity of the body mind. The sense of your presence isn't a thought; presence arises from a place beyond the mind. Thoughts alone have no power. All thoughts are powerless until they are joined by a belief, which is also a thought. Now that you are no longer trapped in the depth of your mind, you have learned to follow your intuition, the language of your soul. You will have made an inner shift of massive proportions. Be aware that after your awakening, your wisdom will be tested.

Now it is clear to you that your emotions are a guidance system to navigate through life. The greatness of your inner power allows you to redirect your emotions to those you prefer, despite any adverse conditions. You no longer place the responsibility for how you feel on the shoulders of others, and you finally realize that feeling good or bad is about how you are relating to your higher self. Your vibration is always your choice. When you are feeling sad, you now know how to take the necessary steps to get centered. Universal alignment of the mind, body, heart, and soul places you in calibration with Source energy.

Because you are making more deliberate conscious choices, you have become a more powerful cocreator of your reality. Living from your center has put you in deeper touch with your emotions and has opened the door to your heart. In your newfound vulnerability, you have surrendered to love. Because you are spending more time in spirit than in the mind, you are better able to follow your joy. This new paradigm has no doubt opened you up to the pursuit of projects, jobs, relationships, and opportunities you are passionate about. When you take on passion projects that move you and touch your heart, your soul becomes engaged and your work becomes your artistry.

In your fresh understanding of the nature of energy, you are now aware of the unlimited power of your nonphysical self. You are capable of generating energy bursts to send to painful areas of your body for healing and to heal others spiritually in their times of need. The purpose of life is to spread love and to experience fulfillment. Joy isn't an emotion like happiness; it is a state of being. We find joy when we transcend the mind and enter the dimension of timelessness.

Because of your higher consciousness, your commitment to your spiritual practice has deepened; your inner light and outer aura have brightened. Old habits and false beliefs have given way to new ideas that better serve you. The pursuit of higher love has inspired you to become the very best version of yourself possible. You have elevated your consciousness and thereby changed the trajectory of your life.

By now you have formed new intentions from greater clarity. Perhaps you have decided to cut your hair, lose weight, stop smoking, or eliminate a bad habit that has outgrown its usefulness. In my own awakening, I suddenly lost the urge to bite my fingernails, which I had done my whole life. In your new awakened state, you have indeed discovered a greater version of yourself. In your new altitude, you have concluded that the journey inward is all you need to create the life you love. Your intentions are creating points of attraction for the universe to act on in order to deliver all you are asking for. You are limitless and no longer see yourself in the world as a victim but, rather, as an unstoppable and powerful being. Through your new eyes, you see a loving world that supports you and responds to you.

Since you have become able to deliberately and consciously manifest, the lag time from the creation of an idea to its manifestation has shortened, and your manifestations often arrive in bundles. In your enlightened state, manifestation is instantaneous. You have become an expert at visualizing your dreams. Your new perspective allows you to paint a mental picture of exactly what you desire to manifest. Each image creates a thread in time that pulls you closer and closer until the event manifests. You have also learned the science of visioning, where your visions already exist in the mind of God. Your patience, dedication, and prayers allow for outer manifestations to take place.

Because your five senses have become energized by a higher state of awareness, you have undoubtedly begun to feel more energetic and alive. You have given birth to a lighter version of you, free of the old patterns of resistance that have held you back for so long. In enlightenment, you just lighten up. You become free of incessant thoughts, labeling, and judgment of other people. The more you are your true self, the lighter you become. There is less struggle in your life as you maneuver the path of least resistance into the land of freedom and joy.

Being spiritual in your truest sense, you now know how to navigate through life by using your intuition. Your intuition is a tool of your soul. You are all things, and all things are you. You no longer see yourself as living in the universe; you have come to the realization that the universe is part of you. The internal path is a journey to your soul. In truth, there is no journey at all. Your soul has been only one conscious breath away since the day you were born. You are a miracle, and the miracle lives in you. Awakening is the process of self-realization and the certainty that your soul is gifted from God. The process of evolution into pure light is absolutely inevitable, and you have awakened to the certainty of this as well.

When you are struggling and feeling tremendous pain, know that your suffering isn't in vain. The scars in life are unavoidable, but the arrival of intense pain also represents an opportunity for an emotional healing to occur. When your broken heart is healed, it is made stronger, and you become wiser. Nothing worthwhile in life emerges without a struggle. You will be tested on the road to enlightenment, and you will encounter many severe storms and heartaches along the way.

Transformation is always a painful process. A part of you must die to be reborn. You, too, will transform like a caterpillar into a butterfly. This process cannot be rushed; it can happen only in divine order, much like your inevitable awakening. It will happen when it is supposed to happen; there is no rushing this experience. Your awakening doesn't happen as a variable of time but, rather, as a variable of your faith.

Higher gifts of the soul include gratitude and compassion. Awakened beings live in a state of perpetual gratitude. Anyone who is wide open inside the heart will always see the gifts life brings to every single moment. Even in your dimmest of circumstances, stay inward and faithful; there is a higher purpose for your suffering. An attitude of gratitude creates a receptive state of consciousness for good things to come your way. Honoring what already is helps you to remain present and aware of the richness of each moment. When your cup runneth over, be humble and share your gifts with those who most need them.

When you are compassionate and giving to those in need, your heart expands. Compassion is experiencing another's emotion as one's own, with the wisdom of oneness. As you widen your circle of compassion, shine your light in the direction of love for all God's children. There isn't anything earth society can't accomplish when it reflects the unity of all loving souls. When ordinary people stand united behind a just cause, their oneness is capable of shaking the earth and bending the path of all creation. Love consciousness is changing the world. There is unlimited power contained in the intention to build a more tolerant and loving society.

As your higher self, you will begin to notice improvement in many relationships in your life. You have become a better friend, a better parent, and a more evolved partner because you no longer listen to speak; rather, you listen to understand. Understanding comes only when the mind stream slows down. Because of your progression, you have increased your energy output, which has magnetic properties.

As you walk the path of awakening, you will begin to feel more love and compassion in your heart. The heart is the home of the soul; therefore, the spiritual path leads to heart expansion. You will find yourself making more heart-based decisions as your vibrational frequency shifts to a more loving state. As you radiate more of the love in your heart, people will undoubtedly pick up on your new frequency. Love reshapes energy and transforms souls. When you serve love from your infinite heart space, your path to a more abundant life is only a heartbeat away. You are love's creation. Your innate vibration is the frequency of love. Love is the way forward.

The more appreciation and skill you develop for living in the present moment, the closer you are to your awakening. As you begin to spend more time in mindfulness, you have learned that any problems of your past and all anxiety of your future are dissolved in the now. Mindfulness becomes the norm as you experience life from the vantage point of your soul. You will spend more time mindfully walking, eating, and working as you sense the presence of the Divine in you. When you live in the now, you gain unlimited access to the love and joy of your being.

Take time in your day to slow down and remain still for periods of time. In the silence that surrounds you, observe the rhythm of your breathing. Take normal breaths in and out and notice your inner flow. Merge with the energy field that lies inside you. When you go beyond your physical form, you transcend the body. This state of being is called *presence*. The beauty of life arises in the silence of your presence. Stay in the moment. Use the now as the main portal to your inner self. A secondary portal into the unmanifested is created through the silence of the mind. Incessant thinking creates mind noise that blocks you from becoming one with the God essence in you.

The key to awakening is to trust your journey and allow your transformation to happen spontaneously and organically. Open your mind to unlimited possibilities. Remain mindful that there is a natural flow to your evolution toward wholeness. Presence is a state of knowing, and there is freedom in knowing. Aristotle wrote, "Knowing yourself is the beginning of all wisdom."

The root of consciousness is identification with the soul. Stress is always a sign that the ego mind is taking over. Now that you have learned how to step out of your ego mind identity, you have become present. Real living takes place in the now. The most powerful instrument against your mind is your detached response to it. Being in the state of thought is like being trapped in a dream. The state of wakefulness is rising above thought. Simply remain as the observing presence that allows everything and everyone to just be. "Who you are in love with is the Self, who you think you are is the ego," Mooji once said.

The real you is your deeper presence, the pure observer; this is your "I Am" presence. The nonphysical self observes from neutrality, without judgment. At the level of the self, you discover great bliss and a profound clarity. You become deeply grateful and aware of the loveliness that exists inside each moment. You surrender to life, and life surrenders to you. The sweet fragrance of awakening is everywhere, and the beauty of your inner soul is revealed.

You will notice that your periods of anxiety, frustration, and anger will diminish as you begin to see yourself as part of a worldwide community united against the politics of separation, intolerance, and injustice. As your old childhood beliefs fade away, new visions of unity and oneness begin to replace them. You will also notice a renewed focus on health and wellness in your life as you begin to realize the body is the temple of your soul. Wellness embraces the practices of conscious breathing, mindfulness, and meditation, which all lead to less thought and a deepening of your awareness.

If you can remain focused on your presence as the self, you can repel the forces of the mind, which will attack you like a wolf, seeking to vacuum you back into personhood. Be a guardian of your highest vibration and inner flow. There is nothing and no one able to take away what is not divinely theirs. There is much splendor ahead for you on the journey of awakening, along with indescribable inner peace and everlasting tranquility. You are wholeness now and forever. Where your attention goes is what we call *experience*. Stay as the self. Go beyond an identification with your thoughts. Be the witness—beyond form, beyond time, and beyond the mind. The real you is the observer of all this, the greater you.

You Are a Soul Born from the Breath of God

Some people are absolutely fascinated with their own story, but
their journey isn't just a story; it is a series of experiences and clues
calling for their attention. If you listen carefully, you will hear the whisper
of your soul calling you toward self-realization. Enlightenment is the
state of knowing you are spirit first. We are all on the road to the
discovery of our truth, but we all travel different paths to get there.
As you begin to expand your consciousness, you will awaken to
your true nature. You are a soul born from the very breath of God.

We Are All Seekers and Healers

Much of our lives are spent learning and seeking.
Our parents, families, friends, guides, lovers,
and experiences teach us. What we absorb becomes
integrated into who we are. We are all seekers,
and we are all healers. Throughout our lives,
we search for completeness. Most people stay on
an external journey, seeking money, power, or recognition.
The greatest experience possible is an internal journey
toward your very soul. The wholeness you are
searching for is also seeking you. The gift of divine light
is bestowed on you at birth, but this is often forgotten
as a result of ego dominance and the distractions of the world.
Remember that you are a powerful soul born worthy of
love, acceptance, and abundance. Celebrate today
the divinity of who you truly are. Your situation isn't
who you are; who you are is pure love personified.

Who You Are Is Love

Who you are is love.
What you are is energy.
How you feel is your vibration.
When you are born, it is called creation.
The reason you came here is to awaken.

Everyone Has Seeds of Greatness

Everyone has seeds of greatness planted inside them.
You must not be disappointed in yourself if you aren't yet
reaching your full potential. Remain open and be patient;
greatness often emerges from struggle. Persistence always
overcomes resistance. Keep working the magic of your artistry.
When you discover the power of your inner essence, the union
of your mind, body, heart, and soul will create a higher platform for
you to operate from. It is from this elevated vantage point that your
greater purpose can come forth and your signature gift can be delivered.

Blinding Remembrance of Your True Nature

As you peel back the layers of your skin, what is revealed is
more powerful than what you are capable of understanding.
Your excellence is coming through. The brightness of your
naked soul is blinding yet magnetically attractive—lightning in
a bottle. There is little you can do to prevent your awakening;
it is coming. What is in store for your soul is a spark of heaven
right here on earth, blinding remembrance of your true nature.
You are greatness personified and stardust from far beyond.
This revelation is astounding yet very familiar. This is because you
continue to remember more of who you are, from where you came,
and why you are here.

Nothing Is Wrong Here

Nothing is wrong here.
Everything happening to you is for a reason. Every action is
birthed from a thought—divine, hidden micro intentions, each
containing the atomic energy of the sun expressing itself
as bits of reality. Your experience is a result of millions of
collisions of your thoughts, desires, fears, and emotions.
This is the infrastructure of your very existence.
By this light you are certainly a cocreator of your reality.
Don't judge a reality experience before it fully manifests.
The result you are looking for is frequently located
at the end of the experience.

When Love Is Your Dominant Vibration

When love is your dominant vibration,
you are traveling downstream in the river of energy.
Divine momentum adds to your flow and becomes your constant
companion. The more appreciation and skill you develop for
living in the present moment, the closer you are to your awakening.
Life is meant to be lived blissfully and meaningfully. Don't waste a
single minute. Every moment matters.

You Are Most Certainly a Unicorn

You are most certainly a unicorn.
There is no one quite like you.
The universe created only one copy of you,
an original for the ages with a love so strong
that you could be made only from
the divinity of heaven above.

Our Greatest Journey Is Inward

Too much of our focus is centered around our desired results.
Each day we grow more impatient as we wait for the entire world
to recognize our individual contribution. Truthfully, how the world
perceives us is far less important than our pursuit of happiness.
You may choose to keep living externally, but to reach your
maximum potential, you must first undergo inner transformation.
Our most important journey is always inward toward self-realization.
Greatness is the descendant of that fire.

Awakening Is the Opening of Your Heart

Turn over the control of your mind to your loving heart.
This is the journey of awakening. Worldly experiences can never
completely satisfy the real you. Underlying this process is the fear
of your ego to share power. Your mind fights to imprison your heart,
because if your higher consciousness gains control, it spells certain
death for the ego. Awakening is the opening of your heart. The heart
is the home of the soul and the beneficiary of truth and liberation.
Let your mind surrender to its divine alignment so that it may merge
with your heart. Simply choose to wake up. Say yes to your awakening
and celebrate the timely evolution of your soul.

Each Day, You Are Reborn

Each day, as dawn breaks into light, you are reborn.
With every sunrise, your yesterday is set free, and today brings
you one step closer to the manifestation of your dreams.
The past doesn't determine the future; it only limits
your possibilities. May divine light shine brightly on
your path, and may the burning fire of love lead you
through every beautiful new day.

I Surrender to the Power of Now

(Read aloud)
This is the path my soul has chosen.
I walk in this direction peacefully and willingly.
I know with divine certainty that with each small step I take,
I get closer and closer to awakening to my amazing truth.
I surrender to the power of now. This is the place where all
things exist simultaneously and where I am in synchronicity
with love itself. I sense myself falling deeper into the realm
where love is everywhere and pure light surrounds me.
The present moment is the window to my soul.

19 Keys to Personal Freedom

1. You are not your thoughts. You are a majestic being inside of a body.
2. How you feel is always a function of your alignment with your higher self.
3. Everything is energy. Learn to sense and feel surrounding energy fields.
4. You are consciousness itself. Your body is merely a garment that consciousness wears for awhile.
5. In order to be truly liberated, you must free yourself of all desires and intentions.
6. You are the cocreator of your experience.
7. See your storms as stepping stones instead of problems or obstacles.
8. Let go of your attachments to people, places, and things.
9. Be inspired to deliver your signature gift to the world.
10. The past and future reside in your memory and imagination, respectively. Freedom can only be realized by living in the present moment.
11. Your soul is limitless and everlasting.
12. Surrender to the moment. Surrender to love. Surrender to presence.
13. Gratitude lifts, shifts, and attracts abundance into your life.
14. The science of well-being starts with your harmony and alignment with Source.
15. The universe is always listening and responding to you.
16. Freedom is on the other side of your spiritual transformation.
17. In order to find your truth, you must transcend your ego-identity.
18. The mission is Oneness with the Creator, with all mankind, and with your mind, body, heart, and soul.
19. Your awakening is your super power, use it!

ACKNOWLEDGMENTS

I am deeply thankful to my beautiful wife, Olivia Fischa, for her love, patience, and unwavering support of my mission from the very beginning. She has watched this seven-year dream turn into reality and has remained by my side through it all. I greatly appreciate her undying love, as it has served as both inspiration and motivation for the manifestation of this book. I am also truly grateful for my amazing family. The loving presence of my children—Flynt Russell, Quest River, Kaya Rose, Neveah Azul, my nephew Isaiah Townsend, and my nieces Sierra and Skylar Townsend—has helped motivate me along this journey. To my nephews—Paul Bateman Jr., Phillip Bateman, and Preston Bateman—I cannot express in words how deeply appreciative I am for your love and support. I love you all.

Next, I must acknowledge how grateful I am for my loving sisters, Sylvia Bateman and Cheri Townsend. Not only have they provided me with emotional support; they have also provided me with guidance and affection when it was needed the most. A sibling's love is precious, and I have been blessed with the most wonderful sisters I could possibly ask for.

To my godfather, the late great, best-selling author Dempsey Travis. He touched me with his gift of writing and demonstrated to me, how to live life passionately. He was a second father to me, and I want to acknowledge his great impact on my life. He was a giant among men, and a tiger in the game of life.

I would also like to extend my gratitude to Sol Aponte, Jennia Fredrique, Eriq LaSalle, Judah Isvaran, Alan Hayman, Sean Collison, Mike Wallace, Gregory Stutzer, Jose Medina, Preston Smiles, Ciara Pardo, and Robert Townsend. They each have provided me with great insight, guidance, and inspiration. Without them, *The Greater You* wouldn't be what it is.

I am also thankful for all the loving friends I have made along my life's journey. People such as Kim Watson, Dr. Tony Clark, Dr. Jorge Minor, Jeffrey Orridge, Mark Thomas, Edward Cruzat, Brad Johnson, Andy Astrachan, Adam Katz, Usher Raymond, Jesse Williams, Brett King, Kenny Mac, Adrian Paul, Cheryl and Sebastian Geifer, Paul Bateman Sr., Dr. Charles DeShazer, Dr. James Reed, and Dr. Stephen Smith have all shown me so much support throughout this process, and I am truly blessed to call them my friends and have them in my life.

To the medical team that saved my life—Dr. Sansern Borirakachanyavat, Dr. Jerry Limb, Dr. James Lau, and Dr. Michael Flagg, all physicians of Kaiser Permanente at Panorama City, California—I am eternally grateful.

Finally, I would like to acknowledge the people who assisted me in the editing and production of the book. Thank you to Tianna Medina, who was my primary editor and without whom this project wouldn't be possible. I would also like to acknowledge Olivia Fischa, Judah Isvaran, Daniela Loaiza, Joanne Medina, and Eriq LaSalle, who each have helped me immensely throughout this creative journey. Thank you all from the bottom of my heart.